FRENCH HOMES FOR THE BRITISH

FRENCH HOMES FOR THE BRITISH

By Andrew Scholey

Published by Wisefile Ltd.

First Published 1990 by

Wisefile Limited

21 Cromford Way

New Malden

Surrey KT3 3BB

ISBN 0-9515861-0-6

Andrew Scholey was educated at Orleton Park School, Telford, and Shrewsbury College of Arts and Technology where he showed a strong interest in Carpentry and Design.

From 1987 - 1990 he studied for a B.Sc. (Hons) in Building Surveying at Reading University. "French Homes for the British" started out as material for a course dissertation, the subject of which was inspired by his work on a French barn conversion.

As part of the research for his book, Andrew Scholey made many trips to France to study building techniques, and interviewed a whole cross-section of professionals involved in the French property market.

This book is dedicated to my parents and all those who have taught me.

CONTENTS

Acknowledgements
Introduction
List of Figures
List of Plates
Map of French Regions

APPENDICES   106

LIST OF FIGURES

LIST OF PLATES

Plates:

1.   A factory where the main components are
      made for houses like the ones in plates
      3 and 4
2.   Prefabricated components at the factory
3.   A timber frame house in Normandy during
      its construction
4.   A modern style show house in Normandy of
      block construction
5.   The cottage in case study (Appendix 1) in
      Normandy before renovation
6.   The same cottage after renovation
7.   Rising damp in a stone house in Normandy
8.   A dry rot attack in a Burgundy cottage
9.   Insect attact in a roof timber
10.   A prefabricated concrete septic tank
11.   An excavator for installing the septic tank
12.   Example of restoration by a master craftsman
13.   Old Quartier of Rennes
14.   The village of Callian, Cote d'Azur
15.   A Tarn village
16.   The medieval town of Perouge
17.   The view from the Pont du Gard

ACKNOWLEDGEMENTS

I would like to thank the following people for their assistance with the preparation of this dissertation.

Mr D Allott	Subject initiator
Mr K Bright	Dissertation Tutor
	Reading University
Mr P Cheshire	Advice on Economics
	Reading University
Mr J V Punter	Advice on Planning
	Reading University
Mr D Scholey	Editing and Translating
D Ackers	Normandy Projects
D Horner-Hill	Horner Hill
N Brittain	Brittains in France
A Cunynghame-Robertson	Cunynghame & Co.
D Miller	Miller Developments
B Newsome	Brian M Newsome
C Quinney	Leamington Associates
A Gooch	Axley Immobilier
K Schrader	French Property News
N Whatley	James Kent Estates

Several other people have been of assistance during my research. They are not forgotten.

Figure 1: A map of France showing the regions.

INTRODUCTION

During recent years, the media have frequently reported on Britons buying French houses. The aim of this book is to analyse this relatively new property market and to provide useful information for those involved. Questions relating to the market itself will be posed. These will include an evaluation of the market in terms of demand, supply and size and what is likely to happen to it over the next ten years.

The mechanics of the market will need to be considered. How do the procedures for buying and selling property in France differ from those in Britain? What French professionals are involved in the process and what costs are likely to be incurred by the British purchasers? There appears to be scope for British Professionals to benefit from the market too and in fact some already are.

Their involvement will be assessed in terms of what they do, how may of them there are and their acceptance by the French.

One of the most publicised aspects of the market is the potential for renovating properties. It would be useful to establish what the purchaser would need to know about the renovation of French property. This would probably include controls on construction such as planning and building control issues. French domestic building technology is also worthy of research; how does it vary in terms of historical development and regional differences?

French francs have been cited in the text when the payment is required in French money. The information contained in this book is accurate to the best of the author's knowledge, but is not guaranteed to be correct.

Chapter 1
The Market

CHAPTER ONE: THE MARKET

1.0   Introduction

The first chapter aims to give an analysis of the market for French houses. The size of the market is still not accurately known. Guesstimates founded upon research will be given so that the reader may gain an impression of the numbers of houses involved.

1.1   Demand

There are several reasons for the vast increase in demand that has been experienced over the last year. These can be classed into headings of monetary, communications and social factors:

1.1.1   Monetary Factors

1.   There has been a significant increase in real income for a large proportion of the population, especially in the service sectors. The same holds true for disposable income despite rising interest rates and inflation. It is true to say, however, that the economy has recently had a restraining effect upon the market. Many agents feel that the result has generally been a reduction in purchasers' budgets as against a decision not to buy.

2.   The recent capital gains on property in Britain have either released capital from housing or provided greater security on a loan for the purchase of a French house. Inheritance money appears to be a

common way of financing a purchase. This has been made available to many middle aged people and in large sums because of the deaths of the first generation of widespread homeowners.

3. There seems to be a greater willingness by the British and French financial institutions to lend money to the British for the purchase of French houses. Loans of up to 80% of the property value are easily obtained and a British house need not be used as security. French mortgages can be arranged in Britain, and with the interest rate being stable at around 10%*, are an attractive possibility, especially as the extension of a British mortgage is not very popular owing to the uncertainty of domestic interest rates. Fluctuating exchange rates add uncertainty to French mortgages, however, the recent declining pound sterling diminishing their favourability.

4. A recent relaxation of Exchange Control between Britain and France and a Double Tax agreement have both eased some of the financial worries of French property ownership for the average Briton. The eventual joining of the European Monetary System should also help. It should be noted that while the relatively low exchange rate has made French houses more expensive for the British, they still remain comparatively cheap by European standards.

* Please note that interest rates will vary.

5. Although there has been a surge of interest in owning a second home, the increasing cost of a second home in Britain has made people look across the Channel.

6. Because many first time buyers cannot afford to buy in Britain, some are buying their principal residence in France. There are many examples of this in the Pas de Calais region, often in the British residential developments, although, in general, residential developments in the south of France have been more popular.

7. There is an element of investment potential for French property but this tends to be exaggerated. Many small investors have been looking to France for investment opportunities because of the decline in the domestic property market and a less buoyant shares market.

There have been price increases in the region of 50% in the last year but these have not been the norm and have largely been limited to the Pas de Calais region. There are fewer bargains left. Although price increases are expected to be 10 - 15% per annum, this figure is subject to many variations which include location and house type. Because of the high transaction costs, short term investment is not a recommended purchase motive. The other investment side of property is concerned with producing an income, in this case the letting out of the house for holiday accomodation. Rental income will obviously vary from region to region. Don't take it for granted that a regular income from letting can be achieved.

A recent article in a local newspaper stated that
"Three major reasons for the unpopularity of
British-owned homes in France were the high rent
demanded, the position of the cottage and the style of
the fittings and furniture." (Mr Chapple of 'Vacances'
in the 'Shropshire Star' 6/11/1989). However, the
cottage detailed in Appendix 1 has been succesfully
rented out during 1989. It illustrates many of the
important considerations;

a) A sympathetically renovated house with many period
   and local features
b) An attractive location with good access from
   Britain and near to local amenities
c) A reliable local person, English speaking, to
   manage the house
d) The owner having any personal contacts who would
   use the house
e) A reasonable rent achieved by having paid the right
   price for the house and its renovation

These factors must all be considered from the outset
if the renting out of the house is proposed.

There has been a lot of commercial interest in all
types of property in Northern France. The main reason
for this appears to be that manufacturing firms
especially are trying to get a foothold on mainland
Europe. This would significantly reduce their
transport costs for selling products to other European
countries. Coupled with this are the lower

accomodation costs for both the production and the workers. Several British developers are currently involved in industrial, commercial and residential developments in the Pas de Calais region. This and the Channel Tunnel are the main reasons behind the attractiveness to the British of one of the most depressed regions in France.

1.1.2   Communication Factors

The application of technology to communications is making the gap between Britain and France relatively smaller, in terms of time, cost and convenience. Improvements in transport and telecommunications have been a major factor in fuelling the rising demand for French houses.

1. Transport

a) Air - The real cost of air travel is falling. With an increase in international trade and more competition, a cheaper and better quality service is likely to result.

b) Ferries - There has been a high level of investment in recent years in the ferry network in the form of improved boats and better port facilities. It is likely to remain the most cost effective way of crossing the Channel with a car, especially on the low tariffs. The new catamaran link between Portsmouth and Cherbourg will significantly reduce the crossing time although the tariffs are likely to be high and the vehicle carrying capacity is limited to 80 cars.

c) The Channel Tunnel - This appears to be having a local effect upon the market, affecting the Pas de Calais region most. The thought of a fixed link has helped promote the "One Europe" concept, but beyond the Pas de Calais region, the tunnel will have no significant effect on journey times or costs. The ferries, especially the Normandy and Brittany crossings, would still be a better proposition. By the time the Channel Tunnel is completed, the market is expected to have stabilised. The only forseeable benefit would be if the purchasers wish to travel to their properties by train.

d) Rail - In addition to France's high levels of rail investment overall, the T G V (Train Grand Vitesse) network is being extended. An existing or proposed T G V link in the vicinity of a property is invariably mentioned in the sales particulars. Travelling at speeds over 180 mph, the T G V cuts journey times to major French cities although the service is expensive. This will be one of the main benefits to the market of the Channel Tunnel; getting onto a train in Britain and travelling straight into France. The high speed route to London and the Tunnel is not expected to be in place until well after the Tunnel's completion, seriously reducing the early benefits of the project. Although daily commuting by rail from France is often cited, the viability of this is open to question because of the anticipated high fares. What is more likely is that people who commute from France to Britain will do so on a less frequent basis and generally work from home. This is one of the reasons for the high level of demand for property in the Pas de Calais region. In addition, purchasers have realised that they cannot afford to wait until 1992.

e) Roads - Motorway links facilitate access to most of the British ports, and the M25 has improved the routes to Dover and Folkestone for the whole of the United Kingdom. As with railways, however, most improvements are happening in France. The French road system is well known for its high quality and comparatively low levels of congestion.

2. Telecommunications

Recent developments in fax and computer lines have increased the scope for people to work from home. It is for this reason that some people have decided to reside permanently in France where they can often achieve a higher quality of living yet not be too far from Britain. Company expansion into France is also made easier because information links between offices have been vastly improved.

1.1.3   Social Factors

There is generally a greater awareness and appreciation of France than there was five or ten years ago. The country has a lot to offer which is affordable to many British people. The most frequently mentioned attractions are:

a) The most diverse and unpopulated countryside in Western Europe.
b) Excellent food and wine
c) Warm weather in the South
d) A relaxed lifestyle
e) A high quality social and communications structure
f) Good value hotel accomodation

The traditional 'sun holidays' are declining in popularity owing to overcrowded resorts, timeshare ordeals, airport delays and unsatisfactory package holidays. A permanently owned property in France overcomes many of these problems as long as the purchaser does not mind going to the same location regularly.

The idea of owning a property in France has received a tremendous amount of publicity in recent years. This publicity has slightly fuelled the demand as well as highlighting what is there to the British public. Naturally, it is not just the British who are purchasing French property. The Germans and the Dutch have had a longer wide scale presence there than the British.

1.2   Supply

There is an excess supply of property in French rural areas. This has had the standard economic effect of depressing prices.

1.2.1 Demographic Figures

Since Napoleonic times, France has had a highly regulated procedure in relation to succession and inheritance. The assets of the deceased are distributed amongst the desecendants in specific proportions. In rural areas this has meant that farms were often sub-divided resulting in an agricultural land-use pattern of small units.

The reversal of this process has been occurring over the last 50 years, leaving many redundant farm houses and buildings. It is estimated that one house in thirteen in France is presently vacant, a percentage which is much higher in rural areas. It has almost doubled over the last thirty years. The French Government has actively encouraged people to build new houses by offering tax incentives etc.

As in most developed nations, there has been a migration from rural areas into urban areas. This has been due to the reduction in the numbers of jobs in agriculture. Since 1965, the percentage of the workforce employed in agriculture has fallen from 15% to 7%. There has also been a shift in the economic centre of gravity from the Pas de Calais region to the Languedoc - Roussillon region in the South. It should be noted that these factors have released precisely the type of property that the British are now looking for i.e. old, rural houses.

1.2.2 Recent French House-Building Factors

France is more than twice the size of Britain with a similar sized population. With the authorities prepared to release more land for housing than their British counterparts, the economic climate is conducive to building new houses. The French are not generally keen on D.I.Y, and do not like commuting, so the new generation of French are quite content to move into modern houses in both rural and urban areas. Since you can buy reasonably priced plots of land in most regions, it is usually cheaper to build new than to restore a derelict property.

The purchaser also knows what the final bill will be. It is well known that renovation costs tend to soar beyond initial estimates. Final expenditure accounts of over 50 per cent of the purchase price are not uncommon.

France's housing stock has increased by 48% since 1968. This compares with a figure of 32% in Britain. The Construction Industry Research and Information Association (C.I.R.I.A.) show in their recent report on the French Construction Industry that France's housing stock is now newer than Britain's. Another way of showing the size of the supply is by looking at the number of dwellings per capita. In France this is presently 0.45 compared to 0.39 in Britain.

1.2.3 Second Home Ownership

It should be noted that it is not only the old French houses that are of interest to the British. The supply of suitable new houses is also extensive, and many developers are building large scale projects comprising both apartments and individual dwellings. Some British agents are now dealing exclusively with these properties.

The idea of buying a second home is already well established in France. The country is the biggest second home owning nation per capita. This trend has been increasing, although there was a significant slow-down during the 1980's, especially in rural areas. This was in part attributable to the taxation policies of Monsieur Mitterand. Also a taste for foreign travel, weaker ancestral ties to the country home, and improved standards of urban housing have meant that the French are now less inclined to buy a second home.

1.3   The Size Of The Market

It must be said at the outset that there are no hard facts and figures currently available as to the size of the market. Guesstimates are the only indicators but these do appear to tally surprisingly well. They have been supplied by British Professionals who are involved in the market. The only way of getting precise figures would be to go through the land registries for the whole of France.

This would be a colossal task. The estimates are as follows:

1.3.1 French Property purchases by the British year by year

1987	-	c 2,000 properties
1988	-	c 4,000 properties
1989	-	c 30,000 properties
1990-95	-	c 65,000 properties

1.3.2 Surplus supply of French properties in rural areas (Mid 1989)

Houses	-	c 180,000 properties
		(c. 1 in 13 rural houses)
Potential Houses	-	c 200,000 properties
		(Redundant farm buildings)

1.4   Imperfections In The Market

All markets have imperfections which prevent them from
functioning at full efficiency. The imperfections of
the French Property Market are:

1. The moving costs in France are high, usually
   between 10 and 15% of the purchase price of the
   property. The next chapter gives more details.

2. The availability of information on property is
   usually poor. This is because the French estate
   agents prefer to take the client to see the
   property as against relying on the sales
   particulars. The transfer of details between
   French and British agents is usually delayed
   because the French are used to a slow moving
   property market. It is common for purchasers to
   buy a property that they did not originally go to
   France to see.

3. There can be problems of communication aggravated
   by large distances between the purchaser and the
   property. A reasonable knowledge of French is
   helpful, especially since the transaction process
   is unfamiliar to the purchaser. The use of a
   bi-lingual agent can alleviate many of these
   problems however.

4. Some French estate agents and property owners in
   the popular regions are inflating property prices
   when they know that a British purchaser is involved
   which creates a dual pricing system.

5. Property speculators are inflating the prices in certain regions by creating an artificially high level of demand. There are two main forms of speculation operating at the present time, long and short term.

The long term is buying properties where high capital gains are anticipated and holding them for a few years. Several British speculators with backing from large financial institutions are known to have bought in excess of one hundred properties each in the Pas de Calais region alone. They are hoping for returns of 60% over three years.

The short term is buying properties cheaply and then selling them on. These speculators are property traders, known in French as "Marchands de Biens". They can be British or French and have official recognition. They secure properties at bargain prices, and normally expect to sell on to the individual purchaser with a 30% mark-up. Since they are not liable for registration taxes, but only for the agents' and notaires' fees, decent returns can be made.

6. There have been cases of illegalities within the market. These include the buying and renovating of properties without adequate funds in the hope of a quick sale, leading to non-payment of bills and fees. Also, the occasional agent has been caught adding either a capital figure to the purchase price or an additional conveyancing fee. In some cases, fines and prison sentences have resulted.

Chapter 2
Buying, Selling and Renovation the French Way

CHAPTER 2: BUYING, SELLING AND RENOVATING
THE FRENCH WAY

Introduction

The French conveyancing system is quite different to the British system. The transfer of title is simplified by two factors. Firstly, all freehold property is registered and secondly the conveyance is performed by a single impartial official, known as a notaire. There are other forms of land ownership which are outside the scope of this work. This is because the British are only likely to encounter freehold title. At the end of this chapter there is a section on how a Frenchman would traditionally renovate a property, i.e. by the employment of an architect and builders.

2.1   Buying a French Property

2.1.1 Estate Agents (Immobiliers)

Before the widespread existence of estate agents, land deals were done privately and on a local basis. It then became compulsory to involve a notaire (see section 2.1.3) in the deal. Many notaires in rural areas began to act and still act as estate agents.

The practice of estate agency in France is relatively new compared to in Britain. Over half the sales of French property are now conducted through an estate agent. It is a higher percentage in urban areas and lower in rural areas. Some property sales are transacted through banks. Estate agency in France is highly regulated. The estate agents are governed principally by two laws. These are the Loi Hoguet Law No. 70-9, 2 January 1970 and Decree No. 72-678, 20 July, 1972. Hoguet is the name of the Minister who introduced the laws to protect clients from low standards of ethics and competence. It is impossible to avoid them legally.

In order to deal in property belonging to a third party, an agency must:

1. Employ someone who holds a charter of property and business transactions (Carte Professionnelle), issued by an official of the Police in the Departement if certain requirements are met, namely:

   a) relevent experience of French estate agency. This is 4 years in a semi-government authority or legal practice or 10 years under a Carte Professionnelle holder. Academic qualifications can offset this however.

   b) that the applicant must not be a disqualified person (e.g. a bankrupt)

2. Provide a satisfactory financial guarantee. This is usually FF 500,000 (£50,000) to permit the agency to handle clients' money.

3. Have insurance cover for professional liability.

The Carte Professionnelle must be displayed in the office and renewed annually. There is a more advanced qualification, a Management (Gestion) Card, which permits the agent to undertake property management.

Estate agents cannot initiate any negotiations for the transfer of property unless they have the power of attorney to sell or search from the vendor or purchaser, respectively.

The Main professional body for French Estate Agents is the Federation Nationales des Agents Immobiliers (F.N.A.I.M.)

The British often criticise the French rural estate agents on the grounds that they are sometimes unreliable and their presentation of sales particulars, their offices and themselves is not always very impressive. The counter argument to this is that rural estate agency is a relatively new profession. It is also very fragmented with many single offices and few chains of more than five offices. This does not help the development of computerisation and more efficient procedures. The other reason is that they are not making much money out of the British. The commission rates are often thought of as being too high but when one considers the capital values, the fees are probably less than would be paid in Britain for the same sized property. This fee is usually split equally with the British agent (See section 3.1.4)

It is assumed from this stage that the potential purchaser has found a property and intends to purchase it. The following process would apply if an estate agent or notaire in the capacity of an estate agent were used. The alternative is a private sale where just the final contract would be signed in the presence of a notaire.

2.1.2 Preliminary Agreements

The use of pre-contract agreements is usual. The French estate agents will try and encourage the purchaser to sign one of these straight after the selection of a property has been made, but this is not essential. The pre-contract agreement can be dealt with by post or fax, giving the purchaser time to benefit from the British agent's advice. This must be weighed up against the likelihood of the property being sold to someone else in the meantime.

Two types of preliminary agreements are commonly encountered. These are:

1. The Unilateral Offer of Sale (Promesse de vente) -
   the vendor makes an offer to sell for a limited
   period of time, usually three months. The
   purchaser is sometimes obliged to pay a 'deposit',
   which is really a sum of money paid to keep the
   sale option open.

2. The Bilateral Offer of Sale (Compromis de vente) - the purchaser and vendor are legally bound by the contract. It is therefore the most used because uncertainties are reduced.

A deposit of 10% of the purchase price is paid to the French estate agent or notaire. This is non-returnable if the purchaser withdraws from the sale unless a suspensive clause is effective. Suspensive clauses, if operative, nullify the contract. The main ones are listed below. It should be noted that if the vendor withdraws, the purchaser gets his deposit back and is entitled to sue the vendor for an equal value.

2.1.3 Suspensive Clauses (Conditions suspensives)

These are intended to protect the purchaser from uncertainties beyond his control. The five main ones are:

1. Non-legitimacy of a sale - when the vendor is not permitted to sell the property, e.g. a seizure order.

2. Non-availibility of a mortgage - this is a piece of consumer legislation allowing withdrawal implemented by Serivener in 1978.

3. Pre-emption by S.A.F.E.R. - an agricultural land commission has the right to refuse a transaction involving agricultural land exceeding 2,500 square meters (2.5 hectares) They then purchase the

property at the offered price. This is seldom
exercised but can sometimes cause an additional
delay.

4. Unsatisfactory planning status - the notaire is
obliged to look into the planning status of the
property. This can be done in one of two ways. If
no building works are anticipated and the notaire
has no cause for concern regarding planning issues,
he can apply for a planning note. This is similar
to a search in Britain, and is less thorough but
cheaper than the second option which is the
Certificat d'Urbanisme (Town planning certificate).

5. Subject to a survey - this is a recent innovation
and is derived from Britain. The purchaser may
experience some resistance in getting it accepted
but it is worth pursuing with an older property.
An appropriate clause might be that any unexpected
defect that would cost more than 10% of the
purchase price to remedy would nullify the
contract.

The following details should be included in the
agreement. This should not pose a problem because
standard forms are usually adhered to.

a) Full identification of all the parties involved.
b) Full legal indentification of the property.
c) A declaration by the vendor that the property is
with vacant possession and details of any third
party rights over the land.
d) The agreed sale price.

e) The amount of the deposit and the name of the notaire.

f) The terms under which the deposit is held.

g) Details of suspensive clauses.

h) The time limit within which completion must take place.

The usual time limit between the preliminary agreement being signed and the completion is usually 60 days. This is often extended because the local planning office and S.A.F.E.R. can take up to two months to respond to the notaire's applications.

It is from this stage that the notaire's involvement is compulsory. If the notaire acted as an estate agent, his role changes to one of complete impartiality.

2.1.4 The Notaire

The notaire is delegated by Public Authority and is primarily concerned with validating contracts, especially those involving real estate. He is an independent professional under the control of the Ministry of Justice and the Chambre des Notaires. The number of notaires are limited geographically, hence the concept of a local notaire in rural areas.

Notaires are also some of the principal tax collectors and are personally liable for any non-payment. They mainly deal with Stamp Duty, Capital Gains Tax and Registration Fees. This means that they will not complete transactions until any monies that they are liable for have been paid. The notaire will also publicise the sale of a property in the local newspaper.

The purchaser has the right to choose the notaire. In practice this right is rarely exercised by the British, the local or vendor's notaire being generally used as a matter of course. It is permissible to use two notaires and the fees are then halved but this is not a well liked, common, or justifiable practice. The impartiality must be remembered; it is not the same as in Britain. Some British purchasers prefer to have a British solicitor working for them. There are several British solicitors who are bilingual and knowledgeable of French and British law. This is a matter for personal judgement, but is frequently recommended.

During the 60 - 90 day time limit before the conveyance, the notaire will prepare the conveyance document (acte authentique de vente) usually known as the acte. This will include the details that are contained in the Preliminary agreement. A draft copy of the acte will be sent to the purchaser to check it over before the conveyance. The notaire will have contacted the Cadastre and the Bureaux des Hypotheques. These are local land registry offices.

The Cadastre is the town planning registry, the French authorities know who owns the land and the purchaser can find out any relevant information by reference to his Certificat d'Urbanisme. It should be noted that the main function of this document is for a purchaser to assess what he can do with the property. The Bureaux des Hypotheques deals with mortgages and other charges on the land. The notaire can also advise the purchaser on other matters such as the merits of the selling price, loan entitlement, insurance details, fiscal matters e.g. local or capital gains taxes, and an estimate of the fees.

When an account is opened with the notaire, a receipt is given. It is recommended that all payments for the purchase are made through the notaire's account. This is because notaires have to subscribe to a collective guarantee fund. Clients' money is therefore guaranteed to be safe.

2.1.5 Land Division

If the land that is to be bought is part of a larger plot, the charge in boundaries must be registered. This is one of the many things that the notaire will organise. A land surveyor (Geometre) will go to the site, mark up the new boundary and prepare the new site plan. It is wise for the purchaser and vendor to be on site with the land surveyor if there are to be any negotiations. The purchaser usually pays for this.

2.1.6 Surveys

It is unusual for a Frenchman to commission a survey on a residential property. There are several reasons for this.

1. The concept of a survey is relatively unknown in France. Occasionally the local architect or an estate agent with technical knowledge might pass a cursory eye over the property.

2. The French are not so inclined to lay liability onto people. In Britain, surveys are often treated as a means of insurance.

3. The French are more prepared to accept minor defects on their properties.

4. The French estate agents will rarely recommend that the purchaser should commission a survey.

5. In France when a mortgage is applied for, the purchaser's financial status is looked at, not the property.

6. When a new or renovated property is bought, there are extensive guarantees for the building works. These are for ten years for the structural components and external envelope and two years for other components. This is a strict liability and is adressed more comprehensively in Chapter 4.

There are no signs of this situation changing.

Surveyors are still an unrecognised profession in France and the British are the only clients that the British resident surveyors can work for.

2.1.7 The Conveyance

Otherwise known as completion, this is the final stage of the process. It will normally involve the purchaser returning to France to the notaire's office to sign the conveyance document (acte authentique de vente or acte) The notaire must govern the proceedings. The vendor and the purchaser have the right to nominate a representative. For a British purchaser this could be their British agent, a friend or one of the notaire's clerks. This has advantages in that the completion date is often altered at short notice. On the other hand, you must check that your property has not been 'altered' in any way by storm damage, fallen trees, etc. before you sign the final contract.

Every detail should be finalised by this stage. This is because when the acte is signed, the title changes hands. The transfer of title is then registered with the two land registries and the notaire retains the acte. A copy of it (l'expedition) is given to the purchaser which acts as a title deed, but is not the actual guarantee of ownership; this is provided by the fact that the property has been registered and the title is then guaranteed by the State.

2.1.8 Purchase costs

The purchase of a property in France is very expensive. A general rule is that the costs are usually 10 - 20% of the purchase price, the cheaper the property, the higher the percentage. This is because the purchaser pays most of the fees.

1. Estate agents' fees

The burden of the fees can fall upon the vendor, the purchaser or both. This is dependent upon the region in question and should be established at the outset of negotiations. The vendor is the most common but the sharing of the fees is becoming more popular. Estate agents have been able to fix their own commission rates since 1986 but despite this, they remain fairly standard. It is illegal for the estate agent to charge any extra commission on top of the rates which must be displayed in their office. This might apply to advertising for example.

The usual fees are tabulated below:

Up to	FF 100,000	10%
FF 100,001 -	FF 150,000	8%
FF 150,001 -	FF 350,000	7%
FF 350,001 -	FF 700,000	6%
FF 700,001	and over	Subject to negotiation

2. Notaires' fees

It has been mentioned that the notaire is responsible

for collecting any taxes that are due in relation to the purchase of a property. Taxes account for a large percentage of the 9 - 12% of the purchase price that is collected. The broken down costs are thus:

a) Conveyancing Fee

Up to		FF 20,000	5.00%
FF 20,001	-	FF 40,000	3.30%
FF 40,001	-	FF 110,000	1.65%
FF 110,001		and over	0.825%

b) Registration Taxes

Land Registration	-	2.60%
Commune Tax	-	1.20%
Department Tax	-	1.60%
Region Tax	-	1.60%

c) Estate Agency Commission

When the notaire acts in the capacity of an estate agent, the commission is usually lower than that of an estate agent, although the level of service is not generally as good.

Less than FF 175,000	-	5%
More than FF 175,000	-	2.5%

Two other costs will often be incurred. These would be paid to the notaire and are for:
i) the applications to the land registry (compulsory)
ii) the land surveyors fees (may be incurred)

2.1.9 Paying for a property

Because of the Exchange Control agreements between Britain and France, the transfer of funds is relatively straight forward. It will be simplified even further in 1992. If two conditions are met, prior approval from the Bank of France is not necessary.

a) the funds must be transferred through an authorised intermediary bank

b) the purchase price, registration taxes, fees and commission must be paid in cash originating from the transfer of foreign currencies or the debit of a foreign account in French Francs.

This basically leaves three options to the British purchaser:

1. A bank draft - issued by a British bank, in French Francs and in the favour of the notaire.

2. A direct transfer - transferring the funds straight into the notaire's account. This is the quickest method.

3. A French bank account - which must be a non-resident's account. Funds are paid into it and a cheque made out to the notaire. This is favourable because a French bank account is useful at a later date anyway for paying bills, etc. by standing order.

The availability of finance was discussed in Chapter 1 as a reason for the increased demand. French and British mortgages are available in reasonable circumstances for up to 80% of the purchase price.

2.1.10 Cash in hand payments

This section has been included because the subject is commonly encountered by the British. It is applicable to both the purchase of the property and also to the payment of the builders. The main points to observe are:

1. The Purchase - This is invariably initiated by the vendor as a means of reducing various tax liabilities. Part of the purchase price would be paid as a cash payment, known in France as a 'sous la table'. This is not a recommended way of buying a French property. The only benefit to the purchaser would be a slightly lower bill for the purchase fees and taxes. The notaire would not normally "be aware of" the deal. The potential problems for the purchaser are that:

   a) the newcomer to the country is immediately in an unfavourable position with the French tax authorities.

   b) if the sale or deal went sour, it would be difficult to enforce the return of the cash payment.

   c) if the purchaser wanted to sell the

property at a later date, the cash payment would not be effective in the capital gains tax liability calculations. The deal would then have cost the purchaser the equivalent of 33% of the cash payment.

d) the French Government has the right to purchase a property at the stated price if it feels that the price is unrealistically low. This is rarely exercised however.

Builders Payments - Work can be done more cheaply by the employment of 'black labour'. The scope for this has been increased in rural areas of France where unemployment is very high. Tradesmen and building companies are not usually keen to operate by this method which makes getting quality work done by cash payments difficult. Guarantees for the finished works (see section 4.2.2) would also be open to abuse. Other problems that could be encountered are points a), b) and c) from above. However, for relatively small unskilled jobs, the use of 'black labour', should not be discounted.

2.1.11 Problems encountered by the British when purchasing a French property.

Problems are becoming less frequent because of the amount of advice that is available in the form of books, newspaper and magazine articles and the British agents which are mentioned in Section 3.1. The two principal areas of difficulty appear to be with people getting committed at the preliminary agreement stage and then having second thoughts or problems when obtaining a mortgage.

French mortgages are favourable but take longer to get than British ones. This is often not allowed for; at best the French are kept waiting and at worst the sale falls through. There should not really be any problems because French legislation offers extensive protection to the purchaser. In making your choice of finance remember that because of changing interest rates and currency fluctuations the best current solution may not prove to be the best long term solution.

2.1.12 Inheritance Law

It is important to seek good legal advice before you sign the final contract for your French property, especially with regard to inheritance law.

Even if you make a British will, French law will take precedence when it comes to deciding on "immovables", meaning your land and property. The essence of French inheritance law, in sharp contrast to British law, is that your children must inherit a certain proportion of your estate. The current high divorce rate and trend towards second marriages means that complex inheritance situations can arise, involving different partners and stepchildren who are all entitled to their share.

There are several ways of dealing with these potential

problems but all require specialist advice. The issue
of inheritance should be discussed and concluded with
your solicitor before the purchase is complete so that
any relevant clauses can be inserted into the final
contract, the "Acte Authentique".

2.2   Selling a French Property

A British vendor would go through the same process as
a French vendor, as is outlined above but there is a
role reversal. What concerns the British vendor is
usually capital gains tax. (l'impot sur les
plus-values). The method of capital gains tax
liability is complex and personal advice should be
sought from notaire who is handling the sale. General
advice is given below:

A. In respect of a principal residence as in the U.K.
   there is no capital gains tax. With a secondary
   residence, however, capital gains tax is payable at
   the rate of 33.33%.

There are many things, however, that can offset this
liability:

   a) the cost of any purchase fees, commissions and
      taxes.
   b) the cost of any improvements and repairs.
      Receipts must be shown for these which means
      that cash in hand work would not be eligible.
   c) a capital gain allowance of FF 6,000 - 75,000
      if the non-resident has owned the property for
      more than 5 years.

d) allowances for the vendor's spouse if the non-resident has owned the property for more than 5 years.

e) a series of co-efficients to allow for inflation if the property has been owned for more than 2 years.

f) an allowance of 5% for each year of ownership after the second year.

B. A loophole was discovered in the capital gains tax laws in 1989 which allows an E.E.C. citizen to make one sale of a secondary residence free of capital gains tax providing they have owned that property for more than five years. This qualifying period is removed altogether where the sale is due to "family problems". There is no definition of what "family problems" is limited to and therefore a wide interpretation is likely.

Finally, a British resident would in any case be liable to British capital gains tax. The double taxation treaty means that the amount of tax paid in France would be taken into account and offset against the tax due in the U.K. The method of arriving at the taxable amount, of course, will be different and the amount of tax due will therefore differ.

If it is greater than you have already paid in France, you have to pay the difference. If it is less, you don't get any back.

2.3 Renovating a French Property

2.3.1 French architects

The majority of renovations in France by the British will not involve the employment of an architect. The only times when an architect is likely to be used is for a survey, for a building permit application (see section 4.1.2), when the property has a greater gross floor area than 170 square metres or for managing the project.

The French architectural profession is protected. Membership of the Ordre des Architectes is essential for entry. This is the equivalent of the Royal Institute of British Architects. The training in France is very art based which is why many train overseas, often in Belgium. The division of the profession is similar to that in Britain. Some work on the large projects and have a high design input to a project. The other extreme is the rural architect. A typical one described his workload as being five per cent art, twenty per cent technical matters and the rest management. They usually work alone, in small partnerships or in conjunction with a building company. Their numbers are geographically regulated.

2.3.2 French builders

The French Construction Industry is more polarised than Britain's. There are several very large companies and over 250,000 small companies which employ fewer than ten workers. About half of these

are self-employed. The renovation of small and mainly
rural houses is likely to involve local builders,
typically small family run firms or self-employed
tradesmen.

The French tradesmen (artisans) have not by and large
formed themselves into multi-disciplinary building
companies; the set-up is still very traditional with
separate trades. Apprenticeships are still common and
are more demanding than in Britain. There is a high
craft content in most operations which means that work
is invariably done to a high standard and
conscientiously. A common complaint of their work is
that there is a lack of imagination and innovation in
the way that they work.

This is because of their traditional training and
insurance cover, which is given on the condition that
they work according to the relevent Codes of Practice.
More details on these are given in section 3.3.1 and
Appendix 8. It has been known for them to get the
British client to sign a liability waiver for
non-traditional work. A noticable aspect of their
work is the way that the tradesmen, when working
within their craft, are very capable of limited design
and problem solving. They take over the role of a
consultant surveyor.

On a typical renovation project, there will often be
seven or eight different trades. A problem for the
British client can be coordinating them because of
distance and language reasons. The tradesmen usually
need pushing to get any estimates submitted within a

month of having been invited to tender.

A month is a reasonable time. As a rule they will not commit themselves to anything until the estimate has been signed by the client. This then becomes the contract document. It is imperative for the client to let the builder know what is required at the tender stage. This may involve the commissioning of a measured survey and scheme designed by a professional for the non-techincal client.

Problems have been encountered with regards to cost, time and quality when the tender information has been vague. It is possible to insert penalty clauses in the contract for late completion. These are often coupled with a bonus clause for early completion. Getting the tradesmen on site can take any length of time depending upon their workload and the size of the job. Between one and four months in common. Getting small jobs done by a single trade is usually quicker. Once the building works are underway, the tradesmen work efficiently. In rural areas they would be used to working together and coordinating their activities.

Small project management companies are becoming more common across France. They are usually run by architects or ambitious, experienced tradesmen and use local sub-contracted labour. A design service can be included and completion dates carry guarantees. This method originated for new-build housing but has been applied to renovation too. Costs for renovating by this method as against separate contracts with tradesmen are about fifteen per cent higher.

All building companies must be registered in the local Directory of Builders (Chambre de Metiers). They must also be registered companies and adhere to any relevant legislation and rules of conduct. The register can be a useful source of information for finding a local reputable builder.

There are several unions and institutions that represent and govern the participants in the construction industry; they are similar to their British equivalents. There is one organisation that the prospective client should be aware of; the Enterprises Qualifees (O.P.Q.C.B.). This is a multi-disciplinary organisation whose members must be both qualified in their trade and accepted by the organisation.

A Certificate of Qualification for each trade is issued to the applicant when the laid down standards of proficiency have been met. All the members are registered. This means that the prospective client can pick a local builder from the register with the knowledge that he would be proficient. Gradings are given to building companies which are members. This certifies their competence to undertake projects of up to a certain size.

2.3.3 The Mayor

The Mayor is an important person when it comes to obtaining the building consents that are addressed in Chapter 4. He is the principal figure in a commune and is elected locally. A great deal of authority is vested in him. This has increased since 1982 when extensive decentralisation of Government took place throughout France. It is for this reason that early and favourable contact with the local Mayor is recommended.

Chapter 3
British Professional Involvement

CHAPTER 3: BRITISH PROFESSIONAL INVOLVEMENT

3.0 Introduction

Many British and French people have realised the potential for making a living out of aiding their fellow Britons with the purchase and renovation of French houses. This chapter will summarise what they do, the numbers of the professionals involved and what governs the way in which they work.

3.1 Estate Agents

The most established set of British professionals working in France. They are usually the prospective purchaser's first contact and are by far the most numerous.

3.1.1 Role

The British estate agents' role is the matching of prospective purchasers with available property. They are not estate agents in the sense in which the term is used in Britain. The term "intermediate agent" is possibly better. This is because they normally operate between the British purchaser and the French estate agent as an introductory agent. This is their core business. Their standard additional services will be summarised at the end of this section.

3.1.2 Functioning

The British agents forge links with French estate agents to create a regional or national French property market coverage. For small firms, this may only be two or three contacts; the larger ones can boast over a hundred. These French agents send over their current property details and periodically update the lists.

Most of the agents have to advertise in magazines and newspapers because they are often small, recently formed businesses working from home. When they are contacted by a potential client, they send an information pack and registration form to them. The information packs vary from being well presented and useful folios to meagre details. The registration form will usually double up as a questionnaire which will typically contain questions about the desired price range, region or number of bedrooms for example. Some agents ask for a fee at this stage.

The client will then be sent property details, either a selected list or a magazine. After having browsed through the property details, it is useful to draw up a short list. The agent would be informed and viewing arrangements made with the French agents.

In France, the French agents usually drive the client around the properties. Experiences by the British have shown that generally, because of the distances involved, it is difficult to see more than six properties in one day.

Properties will often be shown that have only recently come onto the market. It is quite common for these to be bought instead of the properties that are on the short list. Section 2.1.2 mentioned how sometimes French agents expect clients to commit themselves to buying a property after having returned to their office. It also gave reasons why this should be resisted, i.e. because the British agent can offer useful help such as bilingual communications and a detailed knowledge of the purchasing process. Nevertheless, the client should act swiftly to secure the chosen property once his questions have been answered and his mind made up to buy.

3.1.3 Additional Services

Some British agents offer additional services to their core business. This is a logical evolution since the majority of the agents started off after having bought a property in France themselves. Having gone through the purchasing and related processes, they felt that with a knowledge of French they could advise others. Some of the sevices are done "in-house" and others are passed on to specialists. The aim is to provide a complete service package.

The common additional services are:

1. Financial advice and arrangements for the purchase.
2. Insurance advice and arrangements for the property.
3. Taxation advice
4. The selling of French property.
5. Removal arrangements.

6. Surveys of properties.
7. Building works design and supervision.
8. Accompanying clients to France and arranging the transport, appointments and accommodation.
9. Group viewings - parties of prospective purchasers are taken to France by coach or plane to look at pre-selected properties. Advantages to the client are lower inspection costs and an 'expert' on hand all the time. Common criticisms are that there is an inflexible timetable, a limited number of houses to choose from and several people may want the same house.
10. Translation of documents, etc.
11. The arrangement of holiday lettings.

3.1.4 Fees

There is no standard measure of charging the client for the services that are offered. In fact there is a large variation in what British agents charge. This can only be attributed to a lack of knowledge on the part of some of the clients. It is perhaps advisable to compare fees and services before you register with a particular agency. Some of the agencies consistently charge more than others. There does not appear to be any correlation between the fee paid and the quality of service that is provided. The methods of payment are outlined below:

1. Sharing the French agent's commission - the most common method, especially amongst the established firms, and the cheapest to the client. The commission is normally split equally. The principal drawback is that some of these agents are

less keen to deal in very cheap property, i.e. less than FF 200,000.

2. A registration fee - payable when the client registers with the British agent and has been known to vary between £5 and £300. It is usually returnable if a property is bought through the agent. Many agents feel that this practice is justified because of the number of "timewasters". Several firms have said that the ratio of completions to enquiries has fallen over the first half of 1989 from 1:5 to 1:9.

3. A negotiated or fixed fee - usually charged by firms that look more extensively for a suitable property than a typical agent would do, such as firms that are resident in France and specialising in a certain region but without any formal links with French estate agents. The term 'property searchers' is probably the best one to apply to them, despite their being classed with the agents in this chapter.

4. An additional commission - this practice is very dubious and is illegal. Basically, two lots of commission have to be paid by the purchaser. In rare cases, unscrupulous agents have charged a fee on top of what the notaire charges for the conveyancing.

5. Fees from a negotiated reduction in the price - it is usually possible to negotiate a reduction in the price of the property. This can best be attempted

by a French speaking person. Some agents are increasing their fees by receiving a percentage, usually 10% of the saving to the client.

The additional services are paid for in the same way as in Britain, i.e. as a negotiated or standard fee or as a commission.

3.1.5 Rules of Conduct

The rules of conduct for French estate agents were summarised in Section 2.1. The same rules apply to non-nationals. This is particularly in relation to the necessity for any practising agents to hold a Carte Professionelle. It is this stipulation which limits British agents to their present levels of involvement. Two questions should be posed at this point to illustrate how far British agents can go in France. They are:

1. What is the extent of the work that a non-holder of a Carte Professionelle can undertake?

   The 'Loi Hoguet' applies to all people who "deal or assist in dealing" with property in France. It is vague, however, and limited dealings such as a vendor contacting a potential purchaser or a British agent composing a list of potential purchasers or properties in France would probably fall outside its scope.

   In a commentary on a 1981 judgement (Cass Crim. 20-10-1981, JCP No. 83,) a Mr R Boubee stated that "there would be an intervention when an agent undertook to bring together a specific vendor and an eventual purchaser." Then the agent would need a Carte Professionelle.

2. How could a British estate agent legally operate in France without going through the normal and lengthy process of obtaining a Carte Professionelle?

It is imperative that a Carte Professionelle is held within a practice. This can be achieved by:

   a) Buying into or merging with an established French estate agent. One large UK estate agent has recently done this.
   b) Forming a new company with a Carte Professionelle holder who would be a sleeping partner or have a more active role in the business.

There are penalties for breaches of these French laws which have been readily applied to non-nationals.

3.1.6 Numbers

There is a core of established British agents, but only a few have operated for more than fifteen years. It is hard to differentiate between companies and individuals from the adverts.

The author's guesstimates are that there are in the region of 400 UK companies offering agency services. The majority of these work from home with a word

processor, telephone, fax and a filing cabinet.
Because there are no substantial barriers to entry or
exit to the market, it is expected that many of these
agents will not have a long business future, a case of
"easy come, easy go". Older, established agencies
have the advantage of greater experience of the
market, to pass on to their clients.

3.2 Surveyors

Surveying is still a relatively unknown concept in
France. Section 2.1.5 gives the principal reasons for
this. The present involvement in France by British
surveyors has been developed by the British, for the
British, and stems back approximately five years in
relation to residential surveying. Many of the large
London based firms have been dealing with commercial
buildings in Paris for longer than this.

3.2.1 Role

The role of the surveyor is to go further than merely
stating what is wrong with the building. This is less
than half of what the client should require in order
to make a well reasoned judgement on whether to buy a
property. The bulk of the advice given by the
surveyor should be what would need to be done to the
building to bring it up to the client's desired
standard and what this is likely to cost.

Because the properties that are being purchased in
France are on average in a worse condition than those
in Britain, this is crucial. Many have been empty for

two or three generations. The need for a survey on run down properties is being illustrated by the horror stories that are becoming quite common. The main one is that the renovation costs have escalated to well beyond those anticipated.

Few people in their right minds would buy a dilapidated property in Britain without getting some professional advice. The majority of the British purchasers in France do however.

3.2.2 Functioning

Surveying houses in France is much the same as surveying them in Britain. Most of the British surveyors who work in France regard it as being an extension to their British work. Although different building technology is often encountered, its comprehension and analysis is not beyond the scope of a competent surveyor.

What does need to be mastered is getting the remedial works done. Section 2.4 shows how the French building set-up is different. Most of the British surveyors get involved in this, their services extending to project management. Their most common involvement is the elimination of damp and timber decay, installation of septic tanks, re-roofing and putting in additional bathrooms. (Refer to Appendices 2, 3 and 4 for more details.) The actual task of surveying is conducted by the surveyor's tried and tested method. One surveyor is known to make regular use of the standard "R.I.C.S. Housebuyer's Form" on suitable properties. The survey reports are invariably written in English with the option of a French translation. This can be used as a bargaining tool for negotiating a reduction in the price.

It can be very costly for a British surveyor to travel to a French house that is a long way from a port. Therefore most of the surveyors prefer to spend longer periods of time in France but less frequently. One survey a day is the most that can normally be achieved. This is because the country is large and at any point in time there is a limited number of clients within a reasonable distance of each other.

Most British based surveyors find that three to four surveys per trip are sufficient. The best solution has been provided by the British surveyors who permanently reside in France in the popular regions, although they are few and far between.

3.2.3 Fees

Because of the travelling involved, surveys on French property must be relatively expensive. Even the resident surveyors must charge more than they would do in Britain. This is because they cannot get enough work yet in their immediate locality to keep the travelling down. It is usual practice for an estimate to be given for the survey. £300 - £400 appears to be common for an average property, i.e. requiring no structural alterations and costing approximately FF 350,000. Additional fees, paid at an hourly or percentage rate would be due for design or project management services. Surveyors questioned during research for this book have generally indicated that the remuneration they receive from surveying in France is generally the same or lower than they would get for the equivalent work in Britain.

3.2.4 Rules of Conduct

Because surveying is not recognised in France, it stands to reason that the profession cannot be highly regulated. The exact position for surveyors is still very vague and is in fact controversial on some issues. These are presently being resolved. The difficulties appear to stem from wording of European Economic Community legislation and not from hostility to surveyors. These issues have not posed problems for the surveyors who are working in the housing market. "Visiting Surveyors" from Britain are readily tolerated and the few who permanently reside in France have set up French companies and are treated like any other company.

The question of where a client could sue a negligent surveyor is still unresolved. Both the British and French courts have been suggested. The dominant line of thought points towards the British courts. This is because most of the contracts to survey are made in Britain and the payments made in Pounds Sterling. The concept of suing for professional negligence is furthest developed in Britain and also most of the indemnity insurance policies originate from there. It would certainly be easiest for the client to sue in a British court.

3.2.5 Numbers

It is best to think of British surveyors in France in three classes, related to the amount of work that they do in France. The first class are the "permanently residing surveyors". It is unlikely that there are more than four or five of these at present. The next class could be termed "frequently visiting surveyors". These tend to be based in the South of England and make several visits a year. There are probably between ten and fifteen of these practices. The final class is the surveyors who make or have made the occasional trip to France for a friend or to obtain duty free! There could be any number of these. Many surveying practices are presently in the early stages of expanding into France.

Although the term surveyor is used, it is used in the sense of one who surveys a property. Some are Chartered Surveyors, others have other formal surveying qualifications and the remainder are qualified in other related disciplines but generally appear to be competent.

Nicholas Brittain, who was the first to apply for personal indemnity insurance for work in France through the R.I.C.S., has currently done about seventy surveys there. He has probably got the most experience and now spends half of his time in France. The majority of the "frequently visiting surveyors" have apparently done up to twenty surveys in France.

3.3 Builders

Many British builders have realised the amount of potential work that has been created in France by the recent purchasing boom. This has come at a time when there has been a significant slump in house construction in Britain. The builders mentioned here are solely those concerned with renovations and relatively minor conversions; not the large construction companies that have been in France for many years undertaking commercial, industrial and now residential developments.

3.3.1 Role

The British builders that are the subject of this section would typically be renovating houses or converting redundant farm buildings for British clients, to order or speculatively.

3.3.2 Functioning

This section is not concerned with the trade skills that the builders might possess. Its primary concern is to look at the administrative, legal, financial and ethical issues that face a British builder whilst working in France. It is useful to split the builders into two classes: those that reside permanently in France and those that work there temporarily.

1. Permanent Residency - A few British building companies have operated in the established holiday regions in the South of France and the Alps for many

years. They have probably become more French than British in nature, employing and working for both nationalities. Several more British building companies have recently started working in or are looking at working in France on a permanent basis. Individual tradesmen are also in the same position, mainly hoping to work on a sub-contract basis for the British contractors. This simplifies administration and gives greater flexibility to all involved.

The degree of knowledge and preparation that has been shown by the builders during the research for this work appears to be wide ranging. The two extremes will now be considered.

Some builders realise that they are going to work in a foreign country and not just boarding a ferry. This has its implications, just as though French builders came to work in Britain.

For long term success, acceptance in both legal and social terms is very important. This will normally mean forming a French Registered Company or becoming officially self-employed. There are two types of French company; a Societe Anonyme (S.A) and a Societe a Responsabilite Limitee (S.A.R.L) The second type is the most suitable for a small building company because it is the cheapest and easiest to form. It is the equivalent of a British private limited company. The procedure for forming a S.A.R.L is set out in Appendix 5.

The local Chamber of Commerce and Mayor should be

contacted because they can be 'good friends' or 'bad enemies'. It is impossible to work for long without being noticed by them.

The problem with forming a French company and effectively "becoming French" with regard to one's business is the extra expenses that are put on the builder. The main one is labour tax which amounts to 60% of the labour costs, i.e. for every £100 that a worker receives, the employer must pay £60 in tax. This compares to approximately 35% in Britain. There is also a greater necessity to have more extensive insurance and knowledge of statutes and building technology. These problems are all surmountable however and work for British clients could be lucrative.

The other extreme consists of those builders that are not so readily prepared for their business venture. Even a registered company in Britain which is quite common is not really adequate at present. This might change however in 1992. Several difficulties pose themselves in this situation. These relate primarily to taxation and insurance matters, especially if the intention is for the builder to buy, renovate and sell a property.

Working under two taxation systems could be complicated. The company's insurance cover would also need to be considered, having to comply with the French regulations. Extensive guarantees would be compulsory so would need to be provided for. It would be easy to become liable to prosecution. It would appear that these companies plan to conduct all their business in British fashion and be paid in Pounds Sterling.

2. Temporary Residence - Many British building companies view France as a place to expand into but by retaining a British base. The principal reasons for this are to have a larger potential market, variety and as a means of employing slack resources. This last point is significant because of the present climate for domestic building works. Most projects in France will not have tight programmes of work to adhere to. About two months appears to be the normal project period for a complete renovation by British builders (although ten days has been known) and temporary residence is best suited to this. The fact that the properties are not occupied makes this easier.

Some jobs are best left to the French, the main one being the installation of septic tanks because of the advantage gained from using an excavator. Plate 11 and Appendix 4 illustrate this point. If not too much work is done in one area, temporary residence should not provoke any significant opposition from the French.

Several British building companies which specialise in the eradication of dampness and timber decay are now operating in France. These work in the same ways as the general contractors. The issue of dampness and timber decay is addressed more fully in Appendices 2 and 3.

3.3.3 General factors that should be considered.

During the research for this book, several factors were frequently brought to light by many British and French building professionals. These are:

1.   The ability to speak good French - This is highly recommended for any business undertaking in France. For builders though, it will need to be extended to cover technical conversation. Dealings with builders merchants and building control officers will be inevitable.

2.   Building Technology - Several reasons have emerged for renovation work being done in the right manner. These are that:

a) If statutes and other requirements are not complied with, the building control officers will take suitable remedial action, ranging from amendment notices to demolition. There would also be a refusal to grant a Certificate of Conformity (See section 4.2.1) which in theory imposes an indefinite defects liability period upon the builder. The builder's insurance might also be invalidated.

b) A major factor which is fuelling the demand for French property is that the purchasers want to enjoy French culture. Buildings are a part of, and should reflect this culture. Using British building techniques and materials on a French home is not the optimum solution to the renovation problem. It detracts from the character of the building and makes future reselling or letting difficult.

Availability of materials could be a problem for British building techniques, especially as the main source of materials will be local builders merchants although D.I.Y superstores are becoming more common. A good example of this is plumbing materials. The French still solder the majority of their joints in copper pipework. Pre-soldered joints are not therefore widely available. The situation is worsened by the fact that the standard pipe sizes are smaller than in Britain. Importing materials can cause customs problems which are best avoided.

d) Some British techniques would not be appropriate for France. This generally applies to the services and particularly electricity and gas.

Electrical regulations are quite different to British ones. An example of this is that it is now illegal on new installations to have the brass screws showing on the face of light switches. This is not even considered in Britain. Internal partitioning is also significantly different in France. Plasterboard on studwork is seldom used, plaster or clay blocks are the norm. Apart from being more readily available, these cope better with any dampness that may be present. (See Appendix 9. Energy)

e) You may come across a substance called Torchis (equivalent to cob i.e. clay and chopped straw). This is found in external walls especially in the Pas de Calais and Picardy regions, and is tricky to deal with.

3. The taking of tools and materials into France must be conducted in the right manner. The procedure for tools is that if they are to be brought back into Britain, a form must be filled in. This is known as a "Community Movement Carnet". Details must be given of the tools, their value and the builder. The form is obtained from an Export Officer of HM Customs and Excise.

4. Unfair competition from the British could lead to hostility from the French builders. They would then get their countrymen behind them. This is realistic when one considers that there is high unemployment in the French rural areas.

The unfairness stems from the labour taxes which the British builders would avoid if they were not working officially. This feeling is reinforced by the widely held belief that the Briton who is going to take up residence in France, either permanently or temporarily has a duty to the country and to the community.

Payments to British builders and avoiding French taxes which pay for French roads and railways for example, are not considered to be upholding this duty. It will difficult for British builders who do too much work unofficially to remain unnoticed for long. The planning and building controls which are described in Chapter 4 make this virtually impossible. They would then be under very close scrutiny.

Appendix 6 summarises the main points for the British client to consider in order to choose whether to employ a British or a French builder.

3.3.4 Building Costs

There is not much information on these at present. Most builders have not been in a position to realise estimates for projects. The universally held view is that costs are very similar to what the work would cost in Britain. The higher labour costs are compensated by lower materials costs. The problem of costs analysis is that the buildings in question are all so different.

A general renovation cost guide was given by an French architect/ builder. He used a figure of £300 - £450 per square metre of gross useable floor area depending on both the condition of the property and the standard of finish that is required. There is a case study in Appendix 1 which includes the renovation schedule of works and costs. This is the best guide that has been made available.

3.3.5 Numbers

There are only a few British building companies that have operated in France for more than five years. Between ten and fifteen more companies are or soon will be in France permanently and probably less than thirty on a "regular temporary basis". It is too difficult to guess how many are working there less frequently.

3.4 Architects

The architect's profession has done more than most to get recognition in Europe. This has been made easier by a close equivalent in nearly all developed countries. Many British architects have worked in France for several years in small rural practices as well as the large Parisian ones. Their work tends to follow the French architect's pattern which was described in Section 2.3.1. Generally, a British architect would not have much difficulty in getting permission to work in France. Fees are similar to those charged in Britain.

3.5 Project Managers

It is unlikely that there are many "pure" project managers working in France for British clients on house renovations. The British pattern is followed where there are several professions who are capable of the task.

The fees are usually calculated on an hourly, negotiated or percentage of project cost basis. Regular site visits, fluency in French and a knowledge of the French system are essential for this service. Managing the British works is a useful service to the British purchaser when using French builders because

Plate 1: A factory in Normandy where components are made for houses like the ones shown in Plates 3 and 4.

Plate 2: Some of the components.

Plate 3: A timber-framed house in Normandy during its construction.

Plate 4: A modern style show house in Normandy of block construction.

Plate 5: The cottage before renovation.

Plate 6: The cottage after renovation.

Plate 7: Rising damp in a stone house in Normandy.

Plate 8: A dry rot attack in Burgundy cottage.

Plate 9: Insect attack.

Plate 10: A pre-cast concrete septic tank in place.

Plate 11: The excavator that was used for the installation.

Plate 12: Example of restoration
by a master craftsman.

Plate 13: Old Quartier of Rennes.

Plate 14: The village of Callian, Côte D'Azur.

Plate 15: A Tarn Village.

Plate 16:   The Medieval town of Perouge.

Plate 17: The view from the Pont du Gard.

of the coordination of individual tradesmen and communication with them.

3.6   Property Managers

Several companies have emerged during the last year offering what is basically a caretaker service. The initiators realised the problems that confront the absent property owner including security and having a house that is prepared for the owner's arrival. Letting the property can also be managed, e.g. cleaning and laundry.

The charges are usually on a basic weekly fee plus an hourly rate for additional jobs. Grounds maintenance is another popular service. It is estimated that there are probably between fifteen and twenty British originated companies offering this service. Most appear to be registered French companies using local labour on informal conditions of engagement and payment.

3.7   Investors

The term investor can be applied to anyone from the private purchaser who is anticipating a long term capital gain right through to the commercial purchasers who have bought over a hundred properties for a quick sale and profit.

The large scale investors are mainly based in the Pas de Calais region which is where the biggest capital gains have been anticipated. They can make money by avoiding most of the purchase taxes. This is done by being a registered "Marchand de Biens" which basically means a property trader. A lot of financial backing has come from some of the London institutions for this, amounting to in excess of two million pounds in two known cases. This subject was addressed in more detail in Section 1.4.

The general feeling amongst the professionals is that investment in itself should not be a primary purchase motive. Specialist knowledge and contacts are vital to be successful at this. At present a deposit account is a better investment proposition. It is unlikely however that a sensible purchase would lose the purchaser money in real terms over several years. Many purchasers have bought with the intention of renovating a property and then selling it. This is the case for several British building companies where clusters of three or four potential dwellings have been popular. The returns on this are not known at present. The subject would warrant further research when it is more developed. It would appear that it could be a viable concern if the right projects were undertaken. This selection would involve better market knowledge than would be necessary in Britain, because of the vast supply of alternative property and lower purchase and selling prices coupled with similar renovation costs. The renovation of single dwellings by non-builders is not widely believed to be viable.

Chapter 4
Controls and Guidelines
for Building

CHAPTER 4   **CONTROLS AND GUIDELINES FOR**
                   CONSTRUCTION

4.0 Introduction

The statutory requirements for construction in France
are based upon similar principals to their British
equivalents. The two sections are planning controls
and building controls. Although they will be classed
seperately here, in reality an overlap between the two
occurs.

There is also a comprehensive system of guarantees for
construction. These too will be addressed and finally
the main documentation concerning construction will be
summarised.

4.1 Planning Control

The purpose of the planning regulations and procedures
is to control the change of land use and buildings.
In France the system is regarded as being highly
regulated yet straightforward in its application and
functioning. All the laws concerning planning were
first codified in the Planning Code (Code de
l'Urbanisme) in 1954. They were recodified in 1973
which is the present code. The control of planning is
done at the four governmental levels. These are the:

1. National Government   -   1
2. Regions   -   22
3. Departments   -   96
4. Communes   -   36,000

The numbers refer to the numbers of each of the
levels. Only the Departments and the Communes have a
direct effect upon the renovation of houses and
usually only the latter. Plans are drawn up by each
of the levels to show their planning policies. These
are revised periodically. Most Communes have a Local
Plan (Plans d'occupation de Sols [P.O.S.]). It can be
useful to refer to this at the inception stage of a
project to see what is generally permissible.

Other communes work to the National Rules of Urban
Planning (Regles Nationales d'Urbanisme). For a
project to be undertaken, two consents are necessary:

4.1.1 Outline Planning Certificate
(Certificat d'Urbanisme)

This certificate determines in advance the development
rights of a site. It has been included because many
British purchasers buy property on large plots of land
and intend to sell some of it off. Anyone has the
right to apply for one. In most instances, the
adaptation, repair and extension of buildings are
exempt from needing one.

There are two types of certificates, each with a
different application procedure. The first type is a
Certificat A or Normal. On this, the applicant is
told in general terms what can be built on a specific
piece of land. The second type is a Certificat B or
Detailed. The applicant gives brief details of his
proposals and the planners then give their reply and
may also give useful advice.

A certificate will be issued within two months of application and if favourable will give the following information:

a) the acceptable land use for a site or whether a project is feasible in a planning context.
b) references to any planning zones within which the site is located,
c) the existence of any other restrictions such as the site being within the protection zone of an ancient monument.
d) the existence of public services such as roads, drinking water, town gas, drainage or electricity.
e) any rules to follow in relation to the use of land, eg. plot ratios or the maximum height of buildings.
f) the legal, technical and financial conditions that will be imposed, eg. local taxes.
g) the compulsory administrative procedures that would be necessary if the development proceeded, eg. a building permit.

If an unfavourable reply is given, it must state the reasons for the refusal of outline planning permission. Reference must be made to the relevant legislation. This would most probably be the local or national planning documents. An outline planning certificate is valid for six months. This can easily be extended to nine months however. During this time limit, a building permit cannot be refused on an outline planning issue if the certificate details have been conformed to.

4.1.2 Building Permit (Permis de Construire)

"Anyone who wishes to construct or have constructed a building, to be used as a dwelling or not, whether with foundations or not, must in the first instance obtain a building permit ... this same permit is compulsory for any work carried out on an existing building when the exterior appearance or volume would be modified or extra storeys would be created."

(Code de l'Urbanisme 1 421-1)

The purpose of the building permit is to ensure that the National Rules of Urban Planning, the Commune's Local Plan, certain building regulations and rules for fire safety, hygiene and public safety complied with.

Applications can only be made by the property owner and must be made to the local Town Hall. The permits are issued subject to the rights of the third parties. This means that rights of way or light for example cannot be overridden.

4.1.3 Building Permit Exemptions

A building permit must always be obtained except in the two sets of exemptions listed below.

1) Straightforward exemptions - The following building works require no procedures to be undertaken:

    a) fences of less than 2m in height.
    b) terraces of less than 0.6m in height.

c) statues or monuments of less than 12m in height and less than 40 cubic metres in volume.

d) posts, pylons, aerials and lamps of less than 12m in height.

e) any work with a ground area of less than 2 square metres and a height of less than 1.5m.

f) underground operations for utility services, storage or movement.
   (These are subject to other regulations however.)
   (The heights which are given here all refer to heights above ground.)

2) Pre-work declaration exemptions - The following building works require official notification to be made to the local Town Hall at least one month before work is due to start. This is done on a standard form. Permission must be obtained before the work commences but is implied if nothing is heard within one month of the notification.

a) the cleaning and maintenance of facades.

b) the reconstruction of or works on listed buildings (These works will be subject to the building regulations for historic buildings.)

c) the construction of light leisure dwellings of less than 35 square metres to replace similar dwellings.

d) uncovered swimming pools.

e) greenhouses and frames of between 1.5m and 4m in height and less than 2000 square metres in area.

f) any construction or building works that are

not covered above but which do not change the
future use of an existing building, create an
additional storey or create additional gross
floorspace of more than 20 square metres.

This simpler form of planning control was introduced
to speed up the process for applicants where consent
for the building works is likely to be forthcoming.
The application form has details of the applicant,
landowner, plot address, size and ratio and existing
and proposed use of the building. Site plans,
elevations, sections and plans of the property should
accompany the application form. Applications can only
be refused on points of law relating to national or
local planning documents. Permission is valid for two
years.

There is another set of controls on development that
is not construction. Some activities need to have
approval before they can commence. The activities
which are relevant to houses are:

a) demolition.
b) the erection of enclosures and fences of over
   2m in height.
c) the felling and extensive cutting of trees.
d) the clearing of land.
e) camping.
f) extensively raising or undermining the soil.

Generally applications for constructions and
relatively minor demolition works usually receive
favourable replies whereas camping related activities

tend to receive unfavourable replies.

4.1.4   Applying for a Building Permit

Applications are made on a standard form which is sent
to the Town Hall. If the building in question has a
floor area in excess of 170 square metres, an
architect must make the application. It has been
known for architects to sign proposals which have been
prepared by someone else in return for a much lower
fee. The following details are given on the form:

a) the identity of the applicant.
b) the identity of the builder/developer.
c) the identity of the architect (if used).
d) the address of the property and its current use.
e) project details including:-
- nature of the works.
- proposed use of the property.
- density of construction.
- floorspace created.
- height of construction.
- nature and colour of facade materials.
- external woodwork.
- car parking provision.
f) a declaration of the acceptance of the obligation
to observe any relevant regulations.

The forms must be accompanied by:

a) a site plan to a scale of 1:5,000 Or 1:10,000.
b) a dimensioned layout plan to a scale of between
1:100 and 1:500.

c) a section to show relevant dimensions.

d) elevations to a scale of at least 1:100.

e) applications for any related authorisation, eg demolition.

A suggestion is that the proposals should also be sketched onto photographs for enclosure. An observation is that far less detail is required than would be necessary for a similar application in Britain.

4.1.5 The Processing of a Building Permit

An application for a domestic renovation would be processed by the Mayor and his staff in accordance with the Planning Code and the Local Plan. Within two weeks of the application being made, it would be advertised in the Town Hall.

There is usually a time limit of two months for the processing of applications. It can be extended but usually only for large or controversial projects. If a reply is not given within two months, providing that the applicant has contacted the Mayor for a second time a tacit permission is inferred.

Favourable replies can be straightforward or can have conditions attached to them for relatively minor amendments. Unfavourable replies must state the reason for the refusal of a building permit. Reasons must be that the project does not wholly comply with the planning documents. The Planning Code makes reference to the general principles for a refusal:

"The building permit cannot be given unless the proposed buildings are in conformity with the legislative and regulative dispositions concerning the siting of buildings, their use, nature, architecture, dimensions and the development of their surroundings."
(Sec L 241-3)

The National Rules of Urban Planning go into greater detail. It is useful to consider the reasons for the refusal of a building permit because when reversed, they form a complete picture of all the considerations that are prevalent in the decision. The following lists are taken from "Planning Control in Western Europe" (p. 195).

1) These rules permit the refusal of a building permit on a locational basis if it would:
a) endanger local security or public health.
b) lead to development in areas subject to flood, erosion or avalanche.
c) cause a grave nuisance such as noise, etc.
d) be within 50m (40m for housing) of a motorway or 35m (25m) of an arterial road outside built up areas.
e) threaten natural spaces in the broadest sense including agriculture.
f) threaten harm to natural landscapes, flora and fauna.
g) threaten conservation of an historic or architectural site.
h) threaten sprawl into unauthorised areas or compromising agriculture, forestry etc., or the National Directives of Planning.

2) These rules permit the refusal of a building permit
on a servicing basis if:
a) the site is not open to a public highway, or access
   is difficult or dangerous. This can lead to
   parking requirements.
b) the site is required for greenspace or childrens'
   play area.
c) the building is not serviced by drinking water or
   sewerage.
d) the construction damages the environment or
   contradicts National Directives.
e) the services required are beyond current resources.

3) These rules permit the refusal of a building permit
on a siting or volume basis if they infringe the rules
of:
a) minimum distance between buildings.
b) minimum angles of view of the sky.
c) minimum sunshine for buildings.
d) maximum height to width ratios with the street.
e) minimum set backs off the street. unless the
   proposals improve or have no effect on the
   conformity with buildings in the area.

4) These rules permit the refusal of a building permit
on an aesthetic basis if:
a) the situation, architecture, dimensions or natural
   appearance would damage the character or interests
   of surrounding areas, to natural or urban
   landscapes.
b) the buildings do not conform to particular heights
   in partially developed areas.
c) the surrounding walls/fences are not built in

harmonious materials, if industrial or
temporary buildings are not set back and screened.
(Regles Nationales d'Urbanisme [RNU] R111-1 - R111-27)

Few applications are refused if the proposals are
reasonably in keeping with the environment. Local
builders and estate agents will usually have a good
idea of what would be permissible. Another means of
finding out would be to observe buildings that have
been renovated in recent years. Generally permission
is more readily granted than in Britain providing that
the proposals have traditional characteristics. The
French planning authorities are more concerned with
the external appearance than with the interior or a
change of use.

If a building permit is granted, notices must be
displayed in the Town Hall and at the site within one
week. They must remain there for at least two months.
Interested third parties can then inspect the
proposals and lodge an appeal if they wish to do so
but this must be within four months. The building
permit would then be suspended.

Appeals must be based on a point of law such as
non-compliance with a Local Plan, and they go through
the Administrative Courts. It is unlikely that a
standard house renovation would arouse such
opposition.

A building permit is valid for two years, within which
time the building work must have started. Extensions
of this period are relatively easy to obtain. The

permit is withdrawn if building works are interrupted for more than one year.

Should the property be sold, the permit will not automatically "run with the land", a transfer document would need to be used. This is a straightforward process however.

The figures which are given below should help to to give an idea of what actually happens in practice.

a) Only half of the favourable replies to proposals are implemented.
b) A quarter of the proposals involve no increase in floor area.
c) Refusal rates are approximately 5%.
d) Tacit permission is inferred in only 0.5% of applications.
e) Amendments to proposals as a condition of permission being granted occur in approximately 3% of applications.
f) 85% of replies are delivered within three months.
   (Data from "Planning Control in Western Europe")

4.1.6 Listed Buildings

The concept of listed buildings is not very prominent in France. This is even more so in relation to houses. Throughout France there are approximately 31,000 listed buildings, a twentieth of the number in Britain. The two classes are:

a) Classement - The highest level of protection. Of

the 12,000, only 15% are houses

b) Inscription - This is applied to buildings of less interest.

These designations are only likely to affect the renovation of property when the property in question is within 500m of a listed building. Then, any alterations would not be allowed to affect the aspect within the field of visibility of the listed building.

4.1.7 Conservation Areas

These are similar to their British equivalents. Their effect is that any alterations to a building are more strictly regulated. Local advice on what is permissible is easily sought. Any restrictions upon a building in the planning context would be mentioned in the outline planning certificate. The organisation which is concerned with historic buildings in France is the "Architecte des Batiments de France" (ABF)

4.1.8 Lotissements

This is the practice of sub-dividing a piece of land, servicing the plots and then selling them off with outline planning permission for individual dwellings. Planning permission can take a long time to get for the developer but is seldom refused for reasonable applications.

Lotissement is a common practice in France because of the nature of their new-build housing. This usually takes the form of the client purchasing a piece of land and then ordering a standard specification house from the local housebuilder. Plates 1-4 illustrate this.

The factory in Normandy is where many of the components are made. These would typically be dormers and the principal timber-work. A partially completed timber-frame house is shown and then an example of the more universal rendered block construction house. This is on a show-site where the client can see several different designs. The concept of mass speculative housing by a single developer is only found in large urban areas of France.

4.2 BUILDING CONTROL

There are many components in the technical control of construction. One of them, the building permit, has already been addressed in the section on planning because, although some technical aspects are contained within it, it is primarily a planning issue. The other components will be considered under the following headings:

4.2.1 The Control of Works

There are two effective systems of control, implemented by the public and the private sector. Only the first is applicable to the renovation of houses. This is the public sector system. The private sector system is related to insurance cover for building works and so will be addressed with insurance later on in this chapter.

When the building work starts, a declaration must be made to the Town Hall. After this, the Mayor and his agents have the right to visit the site at any time up until two years after completion. This right of inspection is to ensure that the building works are being carried out in compliance with the building permit. Work that does not conform can be stopped by means of a court order.

Within thirty days of completion, another declaration must be made to the Town Hall. This is the Declaration of Completion and states that the works are completed and that they comply with the building permit. An inspector of the Departmental Field Services will then visit the site. If he is satisfied, he will issue a Certificate of Conformity. If not, he must state what the default is. A tacit certificate will be conferred if a reply is not given to the declaration within three months. Over three-quarters of completed projects receive a favourable reply in the first instance and the majority of the remainder need only minor amendments.

(Data from "Planning Control in Western Europe")

Once the building has been certified, the builders are under the obligations of the Defects Liability Period. This is described in the following section which covers insurance and guarantees.

4.2.2   Insurance and Guarantees

France has developed highly codified and extensive

legal obligations upon builders. They are primarily geared towards large construction projects although many of the principles apply across the whole spectrum of building projects. The present system is derived from Articles 1792 and 2270 of the Napoleonic Law of 1804. These state respectively:

"If the building perishes in whole or in part by a defect in the construction, even a defect in the soil, architects, contractors and other persons linked to the building owner by a contract of hire of work are responsible for ten years."

and

"The architect, contractors and other persons linked to the building owner by a contract of hire of work are discharged of the guarantee of the works which they have carried out or directed after ten years where major works (gros ouvrages) are concerned, and after two years for minor works (menus ouvrages)."

A decree which was published in 1967 defines the above terms "gros and menus ouvrages". The definitions and distinctions are:

1) Gros Ouvrages

    a) The loadbearing elements which are essential for the stability and solidarity of the building together with all other elements which are integral or embodied therein.
    b) The elements which comprise the building's

envelope and which ensure its watertightness, with the exception of any movable parts.

2) Menus Ouvrages

Those elements other than gros ouvrages, and they comprise chiefly of:
   a) The pipework, radiators, conduits, ducts and the like, and furnishings of all types other than those which form part of the gros ouvrages.
   b) The movable parts in a building's envelope such as doors, windows, blinds and roller shutters."

These guarantees were slightly amended in 1978 by the "Spinetta Law". Three levels of guarantee were introduced:

a) The guarantee of perfect completion (1 year),
b) The guarantee of satisfactory functioning (2 years),
c) The guarantee required for the decennial responsibility (10 years).

The consequence of these stringent guarantees upon the builders is that they must have compulsory insurance cover for the period of the guarantees. The overriding principle is that the client is never responsible. This means that the insurance companies will always settle claims before proving liability within the building team.

In order to reduce payouts, the insurance companies

have what is basically a private sector building
control system. There are also technical bodies which
check the design of large projects. On large
projects, the insurance premiums will often amount to
4% of the project value. On smaller projects,
however, the same principles apply but with less
vetting of the scheme.

Typical insurance cover for builders who deal with
renovations appears to be the equivalent of £200,000
for a contractor and £125,000 for a tradesman.
Insurance premiums are calculated on the basis of the
applicant's experience, qualifications, track record
of claims and typical projects undertaken. A figure
of 0.6% of the project values over a year was given by
a typical local contractor from Honfleur, Normandy.

4.2.3 Building Regulations

There is a complex system of French legislation
relating to construction work. It has evolved over
the years from national and local bye-laws which were
only codified during the 1970's. These laws were made
by the various Government ministries and local
government. The resultant document is the Building
and Housing Regulations (Code de la Construction et de
L'Habitation) or the REEF and comprises six volumes.

The contents of the first two are shown in Appendix 7.
These are the only sections applicable to the
renovation of houses. The Codes of Practice
(Documents Techniques Unifies) are also incorporated
in this document but will be addressed separately.

4.2.4   Codes of Practice (Document Technique Unifies [DTU])

These are recommended methods and materials for performing the various construction activities. They are produced by the Centre Scientifique et Technique du Batiment (CSTB), the equivalent of Britain's Building Research Establishment.

Other building organisations also contribute to their production. Builders on all levels are knowledgeable about their respective DTUs and are not keen to diverge from them. This is largely for insurance and contractual reasons. Appendix 8 gives details of the DTUs that are relevant to the renovation of houses.

4.2.5   French Standards (Les Normes Francaises [NF])

The standards relate solely to materials. Materials are tested and their characteristics are considered in relation to achieving a suitable performance for various situations.

4.2.6   Agrement Certificates (Les Avis Techniques)

This system is concerned with innovations in construction and is part of the work of the CSTB. It tests new materials and techniques and awards a certificate of approval if the subject matter is successful. It is widely acknowledged in the French Construction Industry that only certified materials and techniques are acceptable. This is because of the standard insurance and contractual stipulations.

4.2.7   Professional Rules (Les Regles Professionnelles)

These   are rules made by the professional institutions
in   order to ensure that their professions are keeping
up   with   progress.   They usually take   the   form   of
assisting   the   CSTB   with   amending   the   DTUs   at
appropriate times.

Conclusions

CONCLUSIONS

The market is large and already well established. It is estimated that there could be in excess of 100,000 British owners of French houses within the next five years; at present there are probably in the region of 40,000.

Chapter 1 gave the reasons for the increase in demand over the last few years. Publicity of the trend in the media has probably played a significant role in the fuelling of it, making people aware of the relative cheapness of French houses.

The general rule for the comparison of house prices is that French houses cost between one third and one half of what an equivalent British house would. The other main contributory factor is the concept of "One Europe".

It is difficult to assess the significance of the investment motive. The general advice from professionals who know the market has been that although the purchaser is unlikely to lose money on a sensible purchase, pure capital gains expectations or the receipt of an income through holiday lettings are not satisfactory purchase motives. It is also unlikely that large profits could be made by the small scale renovation and resale of properties. These projects usually take longer and cost more than was allowed for. This has frequently been contradicted however by "hyped up" media articles or over zealous British agents. If what the purchaser is after is an affordable retreat to use regularly in a country that has plenty of culture, then the French houses are a very good solution.

It is interesting to note that the supply of new houses in France is not constrained by lack of available land, hence the overall supply of houses is not as inelastic (constrained) as it is in Britain which is why large price rises as a result of the increased demand are not generally anticipated.

The process of buying a French house is very different from and more straightforward than in Britain, all freehold titles being registered and the conveyance being handled by one impartial official, known as a notaire. There is also more protection for the purchaser, the practice of gazumping not being possible for example. The British purchaser need not experience any problems because of the vast amount of help that is available in the form of books, British property agents and solicitors who have knowledge of French law.

If building works are necessary on a property, the purchaser has the option of using British or French builders. In rural areas the French tradesmen still tend to work independently so coordination could be a problem.

French contractors are emerging who will manage and undertake the project under one contract but they will cost more.

Many British building companies are now operating in France. Most have not been there for long so it has not been possible to assess their performance. The established British agents and surveyors invariably have said that they favour the use of French builders.

The employment of a British project manager who is frequently in France is recommended for the non-technical purchasers who are resident in Britain and are not fluent in French.

The French systems of planning control are similar to their British equivalents, ie what is in effect an outline consent followed by the requirement for a more detailed consent. The system of site inspections as a form of building control is also similar to Britain. Where the difference lies is in France's extensive system of guarantees to protect the building owner should faults occur. This necessitates more comprehensive insurance cover for builders.

The market has provided many British people with work. For the majority this has been an expansion of their British operations. Their earnings have generally been similar to what they would get for doing similar work in Britain. It is important that the French laws are followed whilst work is undertaken in France. This has not always been considered.

It is difficult to predict what will happen to the market over the next five or ten years. The recent slowing down of the market because of the rises in the British interest rate has shown that it is more dependent on the British economy than the French. This is because the houses are often purchased out of disposable income and with loans.

A general decrease in demand is expected but the market should carry on functioning at a lower turnover. It is unlikely that there will be large price increases on French houses in a short space of time because of the vast supply of houses and the slowness of market has to adjust because of its imperfections.

There is also a likelihood that many purchasers will attempt to resell within a few years because of unsuccessful Do It Yourself renovations or a desire to spend holidays elsewhere will diminish their enthusiasm.

The commercial effects of 1992 will probably remain centred around the Pas de Calais region, and the large cities such as Paris, Lille and Lyon. The southern region is expected to become one of the main commercial centres of Europe.

Appendices

APPENDIX 1: CASE STUDY OF A RECENT TYPICAL RENOVATION

The cottage which is shown on Plates 5 and 6 is near to Cherbourg. It was purchased in 1987, renovated during 1988 and rented out for the first time during 1989.

This example has been used because of the many points that it illustrates. Most of the construction work was done by local French builders and some of the smaller jobs by the owner.

The costs for this are shown. They illustrate the sums that are involved for a relatively small house. A resident British designer was employed for the design and project management. Factors that relate to renting out the property for holiday accommodation are addressed in Section 1.1.1.

DAVID ACKERS B.A.
3D DESIGN, BUILDING AND PROPERTY SPECIALIST.
ANGLO-FRENCH COORDINATION

Le Faubourg, Colomby, 50700 Valognes, Normandie.
France. Tel: (FRANCE): 33 40 30 92

TO CREATE TWO-BEDROOMED COTTAGE FROM TYPICAL NORMANDY
COTTAGE IN SEMI-RUINOUS STATE, PURCHASED FOR LESS THAN
£10,000 IN 1987

COLOMBY
APPENDIX 1(i)

SUMMARY OF REFURBISHMENT COST ESTIMATES

French Francs

A	Demolition, building & drainage, first stage joinery	99861
B	Roofing	22296
C	Second stage internal joinery	41602
D	Electricity	13952
E	Heating	1388
F	Plumbing	19134
G	Fittings and furnishing	35550
H	Decorating and painting materials	4000
I	Allowance for improvement in equipment not likely to be completed in 1987, eg music centre/radio, childrens' play equipment, washing machine, food mixer, barbecue	10000

```
TOTAL OF ALL ITEMS                          FR FR 247783
          Converted at 9.5                  £     26082
                                                  -----


TOTAL EXCLUDING A & B                       FR FR 125626
          Converted at 9.5                  £     13224

ALLOW FOR CONTINGENCIES                             776
                                                  -----


ESTIMATED ACTUAL COST TO LEASE HOLDERS      £     14000
                                                  -----
```

COLOMBY

APPENDIX 1(ii)

DETAILED ESTIMATES

French Francs

A Demolition, building work, drainage,
   first stage joinery:

1 Demolish old stone stairs, old partitions,
   existing floor concrete   7200
2 Unblock windows and doorway   3000
3 All drainage, foul, surface and sub-soil   9000
4 Ground floor concreting   5000
5 Clean and point facade, sand blast
   fireplaces and beams   8500
6 Stripping plaster from ground floor walls,
   plaster chimneys   5000
7 Ceiling and loft insulation   6000
8 Two first floor doors and frames;
   external doors   8500
9 Plaster upstairs ceilings, slopes, walls   5000
10 Treatment of interior walls; plastering
   or rejointing (this item to be carefully
   reviewed after 6)   18700
11 Upstairs partitions, plastered   5300
12 Clearing site and rubbish   3000

                                              84200
        French VAT   TVA at 18.6%   15661

                            TOTAL   99861

B   Roofing:

1	Strip tiles and sort	2366
2	Take down and reinstall gutters	460
3	Rehang sorted tiles on one side	1602
4	Retile second side using sound second hand tiles	3767
5	Ridge tiles	931
6	Finishing around chimneys	990
7	Two velux windows in roof. No.4, with frame (bedrooms)	2493
8	One velux No.1, with frame (bathroom)	928
9	Installation of velux windows and adjustment to roof	2250
10	Jointing tiles at gable ends	486
11	Underfelt	2526

```
                                      -----
                                      18799
              TVA at 18.6%             3497
                                      -----
              TOTAL                   22296
                                      -----
```

C   Second stage internal joinery: French Francs

1	Treatment of existing timbers	3200
2	Bedroom 2, bathroom and landing chipboard flooring	1965
3	Bedroom 1, levelling up on existing oak joists and chipboard flooring	3841
4	Remove floorboards and clean joists over kitchen/diner	2100
5	Kitchen window at rear	1290

6	Kitchen/diner window at front	2185
7	Interior door downstairs (some saving if existing OK)	2800
8	Small windows at rear	760
9	Staircase in chestnut or similar, with banister and handrails	10000
10	Opening up stairwell	500
11	Flooring over old stone stairs	1860
12	Chestnut ceiling on old oak beams	4577

		35078
	TVA at 18.6%	6524

		41062

D Electricity

1	Kitchen/diner: lighting, 5x10amp outlets, light over bench, wiring for heating	2810
2	Living room: lighting, 3x10amp outlets, wiring for heating	1522
3	Staircase/landing: lighting, 1x10 outlet	643
4	Bedroom 1: lighting, 2x10amp outlets, light over washbowl	1170
5	Bedroom 2: lighting, 2x10amp outlets	784
6	Bathroom: lighting, light over basin, power point, wiring for towel rail	1425
7	Outhouses: lights, 10amp outlet in each	840
8	Exterior light	362
9	Fuse box, earth etc	2208

		11764
	TVA at 18.6%	2188

```
                                              -----
                       TOTAL              13952
                                              -----

E   Heating

1   Two convector heaters at 2kw              770
2   Heated towel rail                         400
                                              -----
                                             1170
                       TVA at 18.6%           218
                                              -----
                       TOTAL               1388
                                              -----


F   Plumbing                          French Francs

1   Bedroom 1: washbasin etc                 1150
2   Bathroom: toilet, bath, basin, shower
    fitting etc (cheaper source to be
    considered)                              5493
3   Kitchen: 150 litre water storage heater  1500
4   Pressure valve                            116
5   Mixer tapes, waste                        580
6   Stainless steel sink                      300
7   Materials, pipes etc                      995
8   Labour on installation                   6000
                                              -----
                                            16134
                       TVA at 18.6%          3000
                                              -----
                       TOTAL              19134
                                              -----
```

G   Fittings and furnishing

1	Kitchen units	5000
2	Dining table and chairs	1500
3	Floor coverings downstairs, 40sqm at 80Fr	3200
4	Carpets and rugs: second hand	--
5	Lounge furniture: some second hand available. Allow	1000
6	Allow for transport from UK (duty may be payable	5000
7	Pots, pans, crockery, cutlery	2000
8	Cooker (second hand available) fridge	2500
9	Bedroom furniture: double bed	4500
10	Bedroom furniture: twin beds	5500
11	Bedroom furniture: wardrobes	1500
12	Curtains: second hand available to start?	--
13	Velux blinds and fittings for roof windows	1000
14	Garden furniture	700
15	Double gate and posts	1850
16	Screen fencing	300

All above include TVA in retail prices   TOTAL 35550

H Decorating and painting

Do-it-yourself requiring only materials,
say TOTAL   4000

COLOMBY

APPENDIX 1(iii)

ESTIMATE OF RECURRENT EXPENSES

Annual expenses not dependent on occupation

French Francs

Rates   500
Sewerage contribution (covering pumping
and emptying)   500
Insurance (house and contents)   2000
Garden and other maintenance   2500
Publicity (advertisement in Chez Nous)   900
Local agents' fees and expenses   2500

                       Total   8900
                       at 9.5   £ 937

                                        = 7 x £134

                                        = 42 x £22.3

Expenses dependent on occupation, assessed for year of
high use

French Francs

Water meter   500
Electricity (very difficult to judge but
this is probably on the high side even with
winter use)   4000

```
Small stores, domestic consumables          1000
Cleaning at weekly intervals (42 weeks)      5000
                                            -----

                       Total               10500
                       at 9.5              £1105

                               = 42 x £26.3
```

COLOMBY

APPENDIX 1(iv)

OVERALL FINANCES AND RENTABLE VALUE

Estimated   receipts   from   purely   commercial   letting
policy

Season 1987	Number of wks	Assumed occupation	Rate/week £	Receipts £
HIGH	14	14	160	2240
MEDIUM	14	12	120	1440
LOW	14	10	80	800
WINTER	10	4	70	280
				----
	42 Weeks total occupation			4760

Overall Balance   £

Possible receipts	4760
Fixed expenses: see appendix 3	
estimate	937
Variable expenses: see appendix 3	
estimate	1105
Deduct outgoings	2042

Potential profit per year	2718

Suggested charging for people using the cottage,
per week.

Season	Nominal charge rate, £	Payable in France* Fr = £	Payable in Sterling+	Fixed expenses	Potential profit
HIGH	160	250=26	134	22	112
MEDIUM	120	250=26	94	22	72
LOW	80	250=26	54	22	32
WINTER^	70	250=26	44	22	22

âny winter receipts going to kitty to reduce expenses
*payable in francs at time of holiday
+normally going direct to lease holder

APPENDIX 2:   DAMPNESS IN HOUSES

Two types of dampness are commonly found by the British when they purchase French houses. These are rising damp and penetrating damp. It is not necessary to write much about these in this report because the causes, consequences and remedies are addressed in most surveying books. Each case should be assessed individually. The extent, discomfort, costs of repair and potential consequences of non-repair should be considered.

1) Rising Damp

This is caused by moisture from the ground rising by capillary action through the walls of the house. It is common in older houses because of the absence of a damp proof course (dpc) in the walls and a damp proof membrane (dpm) in the ground floors. To solve the problem in walls, it is necessary to install a barrier. In France, this has most commonly been by injecting an impervious chemical into the masonry.

The second common method is to insert a physical barrier into the wall. This would normally be of bitumen, metal or slate. Both are skilled tasks which require specialist equipment.

It would appear that there is no difficulty in getting a company to do the work. Several British companies are now offering this service in France. Research has shown that the French companies tend to be very expensive for this type of work, the British firms often quoting up to 35% less. Plate 7 shows a typical example of rising damp.

Dampness in floors is also common. This is because the ground floors are often of earth with stones or tiles laid onto it. The best remedy is to excavate the floor to a reasonable depth depending on the soil and its condition and then to install a concrete floor with a damp proof membrane. This would usually be a polythene sheet or a layer of bituminous paint.

Dampness in cellars can be expensive to remedy. This expense would be difficult to justify for a second home. The best solution would be to conceal the dampness or to use the accommodation in such a way that it would not matter too much.

2) Penetrating Damp

This occurs when rainwater penetrates the external envelope of the house. It is usually the result of years of neglect, a very common situation for the British purchaser to find. There are three main areas that can cause problems, the roof, walls and rainwater disposal goods.

A defective roof can have the most serious consequences so should be one of the first jobs to be tackled with a good repair. This will usually mean recovering, using the existing roof materials where possible. Most houses in France will have no sarking felt which can be regarded as a second line of defence. Impermeable walls are not so commonly encountered. The walls of French houses are generally very substantial. Cracks or defective pointing would be the most likely cause of problems.

Repointing, like in the case study in Appendix 1 or rendering the walls are the best remedies. Rainwater disposal goods are often missing on the older rural houses which can often lead to rot outbreaks. It is imperative that they are present and in good working order.

These problems deserve serious consideration by the house purchaser because rainwater penetration can cause untold damage and is most likely to occur when the house is unoccupied. Figure 2 shows the areas of concern on a house that should be inspected before the purchase and then annually.

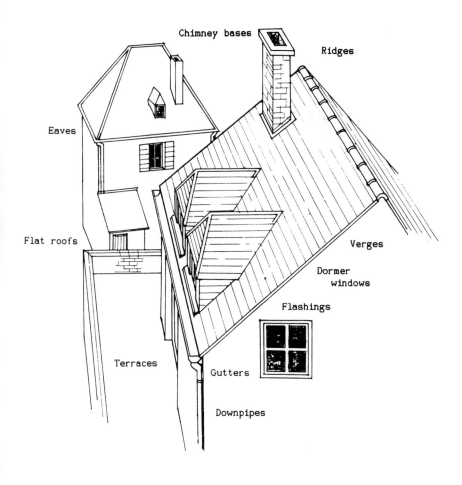

Figure 2: The areas of a house where rainwater penetration
is most likely to occur.

APPENDIX 3:   TIMBER DECAY

Timber   decay is common in old buildings.   The problem
appears   to   be   more severe in France than it   is   in
Britain   however.   This can best be put down   to   the
greater   neglect   of old buildings and the   amount   of
timber   that   has been used there.   Timber   decay   can
usually   be classed as that caused by insects and that
caused   by   fungi.   In   both   cases,   the   causes,
consequences   and remedies are much the same in France
as in Britain.

1) Insect Attack

Timber   which has been subjected to insect attack   can
be   recognised by holes in the surface of the   timber,
frass   (the   beetle's   excrement which is   similar   to
sawdust) and a hollow feel when probed.   Plate 9 shows
an   infected piece of timber. Affected timber   should
at   the   least be treated with a preservative   and   at
most   be replaced if the damage is extensive.   Because
timber   is   more   readily   and   cheaply   available   in
France,   the   latter   should   be   given   serious
consideration if there is any doubt.

The   main   difference   here is the   existence   of   the
Capricorn   Beetle   in France.   This   causes   extensive
damage   but the remedies will be the same as for other
forms of attack.

2) Fungi Attack

The   two principal forms of this are wet and dry   rot,

both being common in Britain and France. These
invariably stem from the presence of too much
moisture. Dry rot is by far the most serious and if
found, should put question marks over the purchase of
the house. Plate 8 shows a dry rot attack. It should
be treated at the earliest opportunity because of the
speed at which it spreads.

If timber decay is discovered, which is more than
likely in older houses in France, its extent should be
ascertained. If it is extensive, the advice of a
professional should be sought.

There are many British and French companies which
specialise in the analysis of and remedies to timber
decay. The British surveyors would also be able to
advise. Remedial costs could add significantly to the
renovation costs.

APPENDIX 4:   DRAINAGE

Many rural French houses that are bought by the British do not have adequate drainage provision. This is because they are not on a mains drainage system or have been uninhabited for many years. Section 4.1.5 states how the lack of suitable drainage provision is a valid reason for not issuing a building permit. The two usual ways of providing drainage are to install a cesspool or a septic tank.

1) Cesspools - These are used where there is a limited amount of space around the house. They work on the principle of holding the effluent in an impervious tank until the tank is emptied. For this reason, access by a lorry or tractor and trailer must be possible.

A local farmer will often be prepared to empty the tank for a relatively small fee. It should be stressed that these are not very popular because they have to be emptied and they often emit smells.

They are also quite uncommon because most rural properties are on large sites. The ones that are not are normally in settlements where there would probably be a system of mains drainage.

2) Septic Tanks - These tanks treat the effluent. If the proper chemicals and processes are used, they will seldom need emptying. The owner should take care not to use strong bleach and should limit the use of biological washing powder. Plate 10 shows what a

modern tank looks like. They are either pre-cast concrete units or plastic versions.

The plastic models are cheaper and lighter, thus easy to transport. They arrive in a completely fabricated unit. The effluent flows into the tank. If the tank is sited through necessity above the house, a pump would have to be used. The solids stay at the bottom where they are broken down by bacteria. The liquids flow through an outflow, filter and distribution grid of perforated pipes where they dissipate into the ground.

The installation must be sited in accordance with regulations laid down by the Departments. They are fairly standard throughout France. Figure 3 shows what a typical installation looks like and the statutory siting requirements for Calvados which is in Normandy.

The installation of either a cesspool or septic tank is best suited to local builders. They will have access to an excavator (see Plate 11) which makes light work of the task and they will also have experience of the installation process. Installation of a septic tank normally costs between £1000 and £2000.

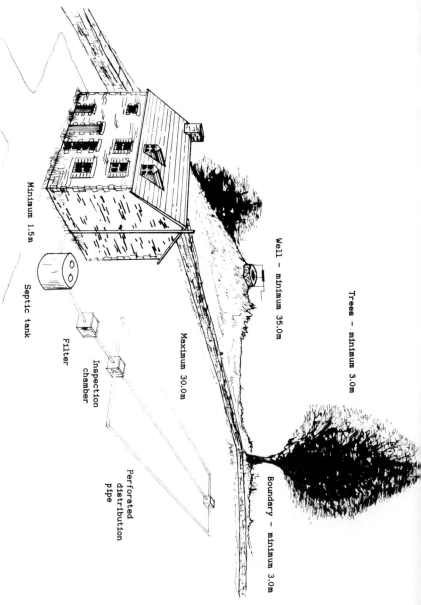

Trees – minimum 3.0m

Well – minimum 35.0m

Maximum 30.0m

Boundary – minimum 3.0m

Perforated
distribution
pipe

Inspection
chamber

Filter

Minimum 1.5m

Septic tank

Figure 3: A Septic Tank – the tank and grid are underground. This diagram shows how much land is required.

APPENDIX 5:   FORMING A FRENCH COMPANY

Section 3.3.2 referred to the need for British builders who intend to have a long term involvement in France to form a French company. The easiest and hence most commonly used type is a "Societe a responsabilite limitee (SARL)". A private limited company is the British equivalent. This type of company can have one director or a limited number of associates. The process for forming a SARL is summarised below. The company can normally become a legal entity within two weeks of application, but it costs more than it would do in Britain.

1) Contact with a notaire - A notaire must be employed to prepare the initial paperwork. The legal documentation for the formation of a SARL is known as the "statut de formation de societe". This would usually cost about FF 10,000. The company would be operational once these were signed.

2) Contact with the "Greffe du Tribunal" - This is the central government body for the forming of companies. It will issue an "extrait bis" which is the official paperwork certifying the company's legal existence.

3) Insurance - Suitable insurance cover must be proved for the work that the company will be undertaking..

4) Bank account - A deposit of FF 50,000 must be deposited in a frozen non-interest bearing account. You can then borrow against this sum. The notaire would require a certificate to prove that this deposit

had been made.

5) Accounts - These must be audited annually and arrangements for this should be made in the early stages of the company formation.

A SARL would normally be established for a 60 year duration. If a building company was being formed, it would be advisable for it to be a "marchand de biens" so that it could purchase properties for resale without paying the registration tax.

APPENDIX 6:   FRENCH OR BRITISH BUILDERS?

The subject of French builders was addressed in
Section 2.3.2 and British builders in Section 3.3.
This Appendix summarises the advantages of employing
either a French or a British builder. The
disadvantages of one tend to be the same as the
advantages for the opposite set.

1) The main advantages of employing French builders.
   a) Using a local builder shows a commitment to
      the local economy. This would lead to much
      better acceptance of the newcomer by locals.
   b) The work would be done in the local style and
      would be more likely to be to a high standard.
   c) The local builders would have a better
      knowledge of the local materials and suppliers,
      often securing generous discounts.
   d) Building costs for structural works that have
      been paid to a French company can be offset
      against Capital Gains Tax.
   e) A local builder would normally be happy to
      keep an eye on a house that he had worked on
      while the owner was away and do any minor
      repairs should they become necessary.

2) The main advantages of employing British builders.
   a) Communication throughout the project would be
      much easier. This should lead to a greater
      confidence and more control for the client.
   b) A gang of British builders would probably get
      the work done more quickly than if the client
      were to use the traditional French separate

trades system.

c) If the renovation was done "unofficially",
there would be large savings on tax
liabilities for the builder and hence cost
savings for the client.

d) The client would be able to pay in Pounds
Sterling, avoiding any exchange rate
variations.

APPENDIX 7: BUILDING REGULATIONS THAT RELATE TO RENOVATING HOUSES

The intention of this Appendix is to point interested persons to the appropriate section of the Building and Housing Regulations (Code de la construction et de L'Habitation).

Only the first two books of the REEF volumes (see Section 4.2.3) are listed, the only ones that are relevant to the renovation of houses. New works are also included in the list as well as other obscure rules.   These are left in to give a complete coverage of the books. It is unlikely that there is an English translation of the Code.   (Taken from "Planning Control in Western Europe" p.243).

BOOK 1 - GENERAL PROVISIONS

Title 1 The Construction of buildings.
1) General rules.
    i) Provisions relating to all buildings.
    ii) Provisions applicable to housing.
    iii) Handicapped persons.
    iv) Thermal characteristics.
    v) Sound insulation.
    vi) Responsibility of constructors/or workmanship.
    vii) Technical control.
    viii) Insurance of building works.
    ix) Common provisions.

2) Special provisions.
    i) Construction bordering the highway.

ii) Boring and underground works.

iii) Private property requirements.

iv) View requirements.

v) Aerials.

vi) Building near munition works.

vii) Building near forests.

viii) Nuisances due to certain activities.

Title 2   Security and protection against fire.
1) Protection against fire, classification of
   materials.
2) Safety requirements for high buildings.
3) Protection againsts risk of fire and panic in
   public buildings.
4) Adaptation of buildings in times of war.

Title 3   Heating and decay of buildings.
1) Heating of buildings.
2) Cleaning of buildings.

Title 4   Provisions relating to the building industry
1) Aid to productivity: coordination of infrastructure
   programmes,
2) Studies and technical research of interest to the
   building industry.

Title 5   Control and penal sanctions.
1) Measures of control applicable to all buildings.
2) Penal sanctions.

BOOK 2 - THE LAW FOR BUILDERS

Title 1   Statute of building societies.

APPENDIX 8: THE MAIN CODES OF PRACTICE THAT RELATE TO RENOVATING HOUSES

The French Codes of Practice (Les documents techniques unifies [DTU]) were referred to in Section 4.2.4. The principal ones, listed below, are taken from "Comment soigner votre maison" p. 93.

DTU 11.1	Ground testing
DTU 12	Foundations
DTU 13.1	Shallow footings
DTU 13.2	Deep footings
DTU 14.1	Tanking cellars, etc
DTU 20.1	Block and brick walls
DTU 20.12	Loadbearing masonry
DTU 21	Concrete work
DTU 24.1	Chimneys and flues
DTU 25.1	Internal plasterwork
DTU 25.23	Plastered ceilings
DTU 26.1	Rendering
DTU 26.2	Paving slabs and kerbs
DTU 43.1	Flat roofs
DTU 43.4	Timber roof deckings
DTU 51.2	Parquet floors
DTU 51.3	Floorboards
DTU 55	Wall sealants
DTU 59.1	Painting
DTU 60.1	Domestic sanitary plumbing
DTU 60.32	Rainwater goods
DTU 60.33	Foul drainage
DTU 60.41	PVC drains
DTU 61.1	Gas installations
DTU 65	Central heating

```
DTU 65.11        Safety for central heating
DTU 70.1         Electrical installations
DTU 81.1         Masonry restoration
DTU 90.1         Kitchen equipment
```

APPENDIX 9 - ENERGY

Energy factors need to be considered in the early
stages of the renovation design as large savings on
energy costs can be achieved if the right steps are
taken initially.

FUELS - The choice of appliances and fuel should be
determined by the mains supply to the property, the
cost of each and money available, the levels of
comfort and controlability required, the property
itself, ie, size and thermal efficiency and the
climate. A word of advice is that although it could
be tempting to assume summer only occupation and hence
a cheaper heating installation, this can be very
limiting later and is not generally recommended.

The three principal fuels are electricity, gas and
oil. They will now be briefly assessed. It is
important that more detailed and specific advise is
sought.

a) Electricity - The French are keen on electricity,
   especially with their emphasis on nuclear power.
   It is therefore available from a mains supply to
   virtually all properties in France, it is clean,
   does not need refilling, there are no waste
   products, it can be programmed for up to several
   months at a time and appliances can be run on low
   tariffs. Unlike in Britain, a seperate
   installation is not necessary for this, it is
   universal.

The supply can however be more prone to power cuts than in Britain. Electric central heating and water boilers are common in France, unlike in Britain where this tends to be expensive.

b) Gas - In rural areas it is unlikely that there would be a mains gas supply to a property. Gas in cylinders is fairly common, even though it is expensive and the cylinders need refilling. Gas installations can be controlled automatically by means of an electric control.

c) Oil - The viability of oil as a domestic heating fuel is open to question. This is because it is expensive and vulnerable to large price fluctuations due to political influences. It is not as controllable as gas and electricity and requires bulky storage facilities.

Conclusion - Electricity is best as it is necessary for other things such as lighting, and domestic appliances and the other fuels are usually dependent on electricity for controls.

INSULATION - The French are very energy conscious. The cost benefits of having a thermally efficient house are considerable in addition to lower fuel bills of course. There is an EDF (Electricite de France) scheme whereby properties that meet certain insulation requirements can qualify for grants and they can also get electricity at a lower tarif. It is therefore wise for the renovater to get information about the requirements from the local electricity board, a builder or a surveyor. The notaire or Mayor might also be able to point to the relevant people.

A recent development in terms of insulation is polystyrene backed plasterboard which is used to line the walls. It is generally unavailable in Britain.

Bibliography

BIBLIOGRAPHY

	Assainissement Individual
	Dept. of Calvados, France
Berengolc M	Comment soigner votre maison
	Editions Fleurus
Dufournier D	Buying Residential Property in France
	French Chamber of Commerce
Duval C	House Finder in France
	Summary 1989 Editions Bertrand
Punter J V	Planning Control in Western Europe (France)
	Dept. of the Environment
Farrant M	Guidelines to property purchasing in France
	French Associates
Holland P	Living in France
	Robert Hale
Hollis M	Surveying Buildings
	Surveyors Publications
Meikle J L...	The French Construction Industry
	CIRIA
Pearce A	The European Single Market
	ASI Journal April 1989
Reid L	RICS 1992 Fact Sheet
	(Issue No.7) RICS
Rutherford F	Information handbook on buying and owning property in France
	Sprucehurst Ltd
Urquhard R A D	Estate Agency in France
	The Law Society's Gazette No 23
	Wed 14 June 1989

Warren L de...   <u>Setting up in France</u>
                   Merehurst Press

The following individuals and companies have made significant contributions in terms of time and the giving of information. This has only been possible because they are competent, have experience and have a good working knowledge of the market.

I would like to say thank you to them by recommending their engagement by those who require such services. There is no substitute for the above attributes, a knowledge of the French language alone is not enough.

D Ackers   Designer & Project Manager
Le Faubourg,
Colomby,
50700 Valognes,
Normandie, FRANCE   Tel. France 33 40 30 92

N Brittain   Chartered Surveyor
"Brittains in France",
Norton House,
New Street,
Chipping Norton,
Oxon OX7 5LJ   Tel. (0608) 644294

A Cunynghame-Robertson   Chartered Building Surveyor
"Cunynghame & Co.",
Martletts,
High Street
Mayfield
East Sussex TN20 6AB   Tel. (0435) 872601

A Gooch   Chartered Surveyor & Project
"Axley Immobilier"   Manager
11 bis rue Porte-Neuve
62200 Boulogne-Sur-Mer
FRANCE   Tel. FRANCE 21 80 31 00

D Horner-Hill   Estate Agent
"Horner Hill"
Wickham Farm,
Hayward's Heath
West Sussex   Tel. (0444) 416733

D Miller   Builder & Developer
"Miller Development Ltd."
Drake's Bottom,
Dirty Lane,
World's End,
Hampshire.
PO7 6QT   Tel. (0701) 32845

B Newsome   Surveyor
Crown Bridge,
Penkridge,
Stafford.
ST19 5AA   Tel. (0785) 713935

C Quinney   Estate Agent
"Leamington Associates"
10, Lillington Avenue,
Leamington Spa,
Warwickshire.
CV32 5UJ   Tel. (0926) 426377

K Schrader
"French Property News"
21, Cromford Way,
New Malden,
Surrey
KT3 3BB

Editor of a free monthly
paper

Tel. 01-942-3946

Due to a computer error, some numbers were printed
incorrectly. Following are the correct numbers:

Page 147:
    Peter Chapman   Contact: Peter Chapman
    Les Campanes
    Le Coblet   Tel: (010 33) 50 44 93 62
    74230 Manigod   Fax: (010 33) 50 44 93 62
    Haute Savoie, France   or (010 33) 50 32 12 54
Page 152:
    Normandy Rurale   Contact: Roy Chapman
    Rue des Quatre Vents
    Monchy Sur Eu   Tel:(010 33) 35 50 89 10
    76260 Eu   or UK South 0892 822181
    Seine Maritime, France   UK North 0860 670056
Page 153:
    Domosystem France   Contact: Gerard Salleilles
    5 Rue Lebrun
    75013 Paris   Tel: (010 33) 145 87 22 99
    France   Fax: (010 33) 145 87 00 59
Page 157:
    KAYA Property Care   Contact: Sarah or Shane
    Rue Principale   Meaker
    Maninghem Au Mont
    62650 Hucqueliers   Tel: (010 33) 21 81 80 12
    France
Page 157:
    Manche Management   Contact: Michael Allen
     Services SARL   Nick Edmunds
    1 Rue Du General
     Patton   Tel: (010 33) 33 51 35 03
    50400 Granville   Fax: (010 33) 33 51 88 44
    Normandy
Page 157:
    SARL Duval et Frere   Contact: Roderick Duval
    Quartier La Plantade
    84190 Beaumes De Venise Tel: (01033) 90650307
    France   Fax: (01033) 90650319
Page 158:
    Delahaye Moving Ltd.   Contact: John Delahaye
    Z.I. Des Amandiers
    165 rue de Bezons   Tel:(01033) 1 39134682
    78420 Carrieres-Sur-Seine Fax:(01033) 1 39134855
    France
Page 161:
    Curchod Continental   Contact: A G Davis
     Chartered Surveyors   (BSc. FRICS)
    Portmore House
    54 Church Street   Tel: 0932 855270
    Weybridge   Fax: 0932 854370
    Surrey KT13 8DP
Page 161:
    David Ackers   Contact: David Ackers
    Le Faubourg
    Colomby   Tel: (010 33) 33 40 30 92
    50700 Valognes   Fax: (010 33) 33 95 14 10
    Normandie France

DIRECTORY OF CONTACTS

AGENTS

Agence du Domaine   Contact: Francis Lesur
479 Avenue Francois 1er
62152 HARDELOT   Tel: (010 33) 21 83 70 02
France   Fax: (010 33) 21 91 89 01

Andre Lanauvre & Co. Ltd.   Contact: Mr J C G Andre
9 Old Bond Street
London   Tel: 071 499 0587
W1X 3TA   Fax: 071 493 5329

Appleby & Sons   Contact: Paul Appleby
54 Kensington Place
Brighton   Tel: 0273 680900
Sussex BN1 4EJ   Fax: 0273 679278

Aquitaine Associates   Contact: Dick Price
Les Joubins
La Roquille   Tel: (010 33) 57 41 23 56
33220 Ste Foy La Grande   Fax: (010 33) 57 41 24 38
France

Barbers Estate Agents   Contact: Miles Barber
427-429 North End Road
Fulham   Tel: 071 381 0112
London   Fax: 071 385 9144
SW6 1NX

Peter Chapman   Contact: Peter Chapman
Les Campanes
Le Coblet   Tel: (010 33) 50 44 93 66
74230 Manigod   Fax: (010 33) 50 44 93 62
Haute Savoie, France   or (010 33) 50 32 12 54

Donald Dunn & Associates   Contact: D W Dunn FRICS
6 Royal Chase
Tunbridge Wells   Tel: 0892 548988
Kent   Fax: 0892 510599
TN4 8AY

Farrar Stead & Glyn   Contact: Beatrice Braud
656 Fulham Road
London   Tel: 071 731 4391
SW6 5RX   Fax: 071 736 9816
                                 Telex: 295845 FS&G

Finch in France   Contact: French Desk
Waddington House
The Street   Tel: 0297 60755
Charmouth   Fax: 0297 60415
Dorset DT6 6QE

Francophiles Limited   Contact: Liz Oliver
Barker Chambers
Barker Road   Tel: 0622 688165
Maidstone   Fax: 0622 671840
Kent ME16 8SF   Telex: 96326

The French Property Shop   Contact: Sally Treganowan
Wadhurst Road
Mark Cross   Tel: 0892 852449
East Sussex
TN6 3PB

Gerrard & Gerrard Limited Contact: Antony Gerrard
280 Earls Court Road
London   Tel: 071 370 4001
SW5 9AS   Fax: 071 835 1436

Hamptons International   Contact: Caroline Peal
6 Arlington Street
St James'   Tel: 071 493 8222
London   Fax: 071 493 4921
SW1A 1RB   Telex: 25341

Immobilier Campedel   Contact: M. Campedel
Rue Nationale
32110 Nogaro   Tel: (010 33) 62 69 01 00
Gascony   Fax: (010 33) 62 69 08 65
France

James Kent Estates   Contact: Nicholas Whatle
Glyde's Farm
Ashburnham   Tel: 0323 833854
Nr Battle   Fax: 0323 833854
East Sussex TN33 9PB

Latitudes Limited   Contact: Penny Zoldan
14 Pipers Green Lane
Edgware   Tel: 081 958 5485
Middlesex HA8 8DG   Fax: 081 958 6381

Leamington Associates   Contact: Colin Quinney
10 Lillington Avenue
Leamington Spa   Tel: 0926 426377
Warwickshire   Fax: 0926 831206
CV32 5UJ

Maison D'Etre   Contact: Pierre Marcar
35 Elmfield Mansions
Elmfield Road   Tel: 081 771 1233
London
SW17 8AA

Northern France   Contact: Vivian Bridge
   Properties Limited
70 Brewer Street   Tel: 071 287 4940
London   Fax: 071 287 3712
W1R 3PJ

Overseas Property Shop   Contact: Mr Bob Jones
48 High Street
Camberley   Tel: 0276 686696
Surrey   Fax: 0276 686636
GU15

Property France   Contact: Gill Richards/
A Division of Charles,   Sue Cox
Lucas Marshall Solicitors
Portway   Tel: 0235 772211
Wantage, Oxon OX12 9BU   Fax: 0235 772234

```
Properties in France        Contact: Mr J C Carter
Les Loges
La Breille les Pins         Tel: (010 33) 41 52 02 18
49390 Vernantes             Fax: (010 33) 41 52 02 47
France


Richmond French Properties  Contact: Mrs Marie-Joell
Richmond House                       Trembath/Mrs
94 High Street                       Annie Palmer
Needham Market              Tel: 0449 722432
Suffolk IP6 8DG             Fax: 0449 720971


Tavnerstar Limited          Contact: Martin Steele
Dominic House
171 - 177 London Road       Tel: 081 549 4251
Kingston Upon Thames        Fax: 081 546 5222
Surrey                      Telex: 918417 STARAD G
KT2 6RA


Villas Abroad Properties    Contact: Mrs A Y Adler
  Golf Consultants
55 York Street              Tel: 081 891 5444
Twickenham                  Fax: 081 892 0204
Middlesex TW1 3LL
```

AGENTS FOR NEW PROPERTIES

```
Mills & Co.                    Contact: John Turner
The Annexe
The Eades                      Tel: 06846 3921
Upton Upon Severn                or 06846 4588
Worcestershire                 Fax: 06846 4425
WR8 0QN                        Telex: 9401102 MILS G
```

ARCHITECTS

Quest International
  France S.A.
3-5 Boulevard de Courbevoie
92200 Neuilly-sur-Seine
Ile de la Jatte
Paris France

Contact: Jean-Jaques
            Senard

Tel: (010 33) 147452788
Fax: (010 33) 147453009
Telex: UK 3518 Questa G

BUILDERS

David Ackers, Designer
Le Faubourg
Colomby
50700 Valognes
Normandie France

Contact: David Ackers

Tel: (010 33) 33 40 30 92
Fax: (010 33) 33 95 14 10

Aquitaine Associates
Les Joubins
La Roquille
33220 Ste Foy La Grande
France

Contact: Dick Price

Tel: (010 33) 57 41 23 56
Fax: (010 33) 57 41 24 38

Axley SARL
Chartered Surveyors
22 Rue de Petit Bois Hure
Boisjean
62170 Montreuil-Sur-Mer
France

Contact: Alex Gooch
        BSc A.R.I.C.S.

Tel: 081 748 2198
  or (010 33) 21 81 47 96

European
Property Restorations   Contact: P S Ward/JP
East Knighton Farm   Jordan (Partners)
East Knighton
Nr Dorchester   Tel: 0202 304840
Dorset DT2 8LG

Maison Individuelle   Contact: Gordon Roughan
Contract House
27 Hyde Way   Tel: 0707 376255
Welwyn Garden City   Fax: 0707 376250
Herts AL7 3UQ

Normandie Rurale   Contact: Roy Chapman
Rue des Quatre Vents
Monchy Sur Eu   Tel: (010 33) 35 50 89 10
76260 Eu   or UK South 0892 82218
Seine Maritime, France   UK North 0860 67005

Planned Appearances Ltd   Contact: Nicholas Snelling
7 Holmlea Court
Chatsworth Road   Tel: 081 677 3033
Croydon   or 081 688 4204
CRO 1HA

Solaris   Contact:Christine Johnston
11 Fitzroy Road
London NW1 8TU   Tel: 071 722 3352
   - or -   Fax: 071 586 3613
18 Ave des Champs Elysees
Paris, France

DAMP PROOFING/TIMBER TREATMENTS

Domosystem-France   Contact:Gerard Salleilles
5 Rue Lebrun
75013 Paris   Tel: (010 33) 145 87 22
France   Fax: (010 33) 145 87 00

FINANCE

Banque Transatlantique   Contact: Brigitte
103 Mount Street   Vandenabeele
London
W1Y 5HE   Tel: 071 493 6717
                                  Fax: 071 495 1018

BNP Mortgages Limited   Contact: Mr J Warlow
Knollys House
47 Mark Lane   Tel: 071 929 4002
London   Fax: 071 283 0238
EC3R 7QH   Telex: 8811253 BNPM

Credit Agricole   Contact: E Demalden
14 St Paul's Churchyard
London   Tel: 071 248 1400
EC4M 8BD   Fax: 071 248 0788
                                  Telex: 8811521

Equity and Life Assurance   Contact: Marketing
  Society Limited   (Mortgages - Support)
Amersham Road
High Wycombe   Tel: 0494 463463
Bucks   Fax: 0494 471915
HP13 6BU   Telex: 83385

```
Leamington Associates          Contact:Colin Quinney
10 Lillington Avenue
Leamington Spa                 Tel: 0926 426377
Warwickshire                   Fax: 0926 831206
CV32 5UJ


Legal & General                Contact: Simon Conn
51/53 Church Road
Hove                           Tel: 0273 746060
Sussex                         Fax: 0273 220921
BN3 2BD


South Eastern Financial        Contact:Mr V Eacott
  Services/France Scene Property
The Variety Centre             Tel: 0634 844442
Unit 68/9                        or 0634 844443
270-272 High Street            Fax: 0634 844585
Chatham
Kent   ME4 3BP
```

INSURANCE

```
Holiday Insurance Services     Contact: Brian Sharp
  (Homes) Limited
218 Main Road                  Tel: 0708 745196
Gidea Park                     Fax: 0708 742524
Romford
Essex   RM2 5JD


Homes Abroad Insurance         Contact: Paul Shieber
98 Bromham Road
Bedford                        Tel: 0234 273533
MK40 2QH                       Fax: 0604 28194
```

LEGAL

Alan T Jenkins & Co.   Contact: Alan T Jenkins
36a King Street
Carmathen   Tel: 0267 235019
Dyfed   Fax: 0267 236690
South Wales SA31 1BS

Bennett & Bennett   Contact: Trevor Bennett
Bridge House
2 Heyes Lane   Tel: 0625 586937
Alderley Edge   Fax: 0625 585362
Cheshire SK9 7JY   Telex: 665556

Blake Lapthorn   Contact: Michael Profit
1 Stoke Road
Gosport   Tel: 0705 510161
Hampshire   Fax: 0705 510188
PO12 1LU

Bookers and Bolton   Contact: R Wisaac
5 Vicarage Hill
Alton   Tel: 0420 82881
Hampshire   Fax: 0420 89880
GU34

B P Collins & Co.   Contact: P D Wilkinson
South Bank Chambers   (Notary Public)
Gerrards Cross
Buckinghamshire   Tel: 0753 888329
SL9 8BR   Fax: 0753 880234

Roslyn Innocent
Belfort le Haut
Fonters du Razes
11400 Castelnaudary
France

Contact: Roslyn Innocent

Tel: (010 33) 68 60 52 17
Fax: (010 33) 68 60 52 26

Sean O'Connor & Co.
113 High Street
Tonbridge
Kent TN9 1DL

Contact: Sean O'Connor

Tel: 0732 365378
Fax: 0732 365378

Pannone Blackburn
123 Deansgate
Manchester
M3 2BU

Contact:Mauricette
            Sheurer
Tel: 061 832 3000 ext 310
Fax: 061 839 2471

Russell-Cooke Potter &
  Chapman
11 Old Square
Lincoln's Hill
London   WC2A 3TS

Contact: Sally Osborne

Tel: 071 405 6566
Fax: 071 831 2565
Telex: 266147

Thompson Quarrell
35 Essex Street
London
WC2R 3BE

Contact: Mr P C Calvert

Tel: 071 353 5703
Fax: 071 353 3981
Telex: 883241

Vizards
42/3 Bedford Row
London
WC1R 4LL

Contact:Micheal P D Ellman

Tel: 071 405 6302
Fax: 071 405 6248
Telex: 261045

PROPERTY MINDING AND MAINTENANCE

KAYA Property Care
Rue Principale
Maininghem Au Mont
62650 Hucqueliers
France

Contact: Sarah or Shane
Meaker

Tel: (010 33) 21 81 80

Manche Management
  Services SARL
- Normandy Link -
Place de L'Eglise
50740 CAROLLES
Normandy

Contact: Michael Allen
Nick Edmunds

Tel: (010 33) 33 51 35
Fax: (010 33) 33 51 88

Calville Property
  Services SARL
La Ferme des Vallots
Route D'Orbec
14140 Livarot
Normandie

Contact: Andrew Wright

Tel: (010 33) 31320497

PROPERTY PURCHASE AND SALE CONSULTANTS

SARL Duval et Frere
Quartier La Plantade
84190 Beaumes De Venise
France

Contact: Roderick Duval

Tel: (010 33) 9065030
Fax: (010 33) 9065031

REMOVALS

Corfield Limited   Contact: Maria Almack
14 Queensway
Stem Lane   Tel: 0425 621172
New Milton   Fax: 0425 638479
Hampshire   BH25 5NN   Telex: 417140

- Also at -

Corfield Limited   Contact: Lynda Sagin
Rennel House
Mill Place   Tel: 081 547 2233
Kingston Upon Thames   Fax: 081 547 3831
Surrey   KT1 2RL

Delahaye Moving Limited   Contact: John Delahaye
Unit 7
Kimpton Industrial Estate   Tel: 081 641 7300
Kimpton Road   Fax: 081 641 5102
Sutton Surrey   SM3 9QP

- Also at -

Delahaye Moving Limited   Contact: John Delahaye
Z.I. Des Amandiers
165 rue de Bezons   Tel: (01033) 139134
78420 Carrieres-Sur-Seine   Fax: (01033) 139134
France

Flair International   Contact: Jim Witham
9 Park Road
Bexhill on Sea   Tel: 0424 215380
East Sussex   Fax: 0424 218520
TN39 3HY

G B Transport   Contact: G M Brown
Oakley Green
Windsor   Tel: 0753 866481
Berkshire   Fax: 0753 830665
SL4 4PZ   Telex: 846559

Mark Alan Removal Services   Contact: Mark Brett
19 St Georges Square
Maidstone   Tel: 0892 73624
Kent   or 0622 758471
ME16 8JR   Fax: 0622 685114

The Old House (Removals &   Contact: Keith Steele
  Warehouseing) Limited
88 Worple Road   Tel: 081 947 1817
Wimbledon   Fax: 0323 894474
London SW19 4HZ   Telex: 87638

Rings International Movers   Contact: Tony Richman
A division of Richman Ring Ltd.
Princes Street   Tel: 0795 427151
Sittingbourne   or 0795 427152
Kent   Fax: 0795 428804
ME10 3HH   Telex: 96291 RING-G

Trenchards International   Contact: Robert Durell
543 Wallisdown Road
Poole   Tel: 0202 510235
Dorset   Fax: 0202 521477
BH12 5AD   Telex: 417184

White & Co. PLC   Contact: K Seale
Invincible Road
Farnborough   Tel: 0252 541674
Hampshire   Fax: 0252 376140
(Branches Nationwide)   Telex: 858905

SANITARY FACILITIES

Swedal (UK) Limited   Contact: Alan Turner
P O Box 10
'Camberley   Tel: 0252 890427
Surrey   Fax: 0252 870525
GU17 7XQ   Telex: 859539

SURVEYORS

Nicholas Brittain   Contact: N Brittain
Norton House
New Street   Tel: 0608 644294
Chipping Norton   Fax: 0608 641728
Oxon   OX7 5LJ

                    - also known as -

Brittains in France   Contact: N Brittain
Rue Anne de Bretagne
56220 Malansac   Tel: (010 33) 97 66 14 78
France   Fax: (010 33) 97 66 14 77

Cunynghame & Co.   Contact: Mr A J
Martletts   Cunynghame-Robertson
High Street
Mayfield   Tel: 0435 872601
East Sussex TN20 6AB   Fax: 0435 872074

Curchod Continental   Contact: A G Davis
 Chartered Surveyors   (BSc FRICS)
Portmore House
54 Church Street
Weybridge
Surrey KT13 8DP

John Warwick & Assoc.   Contact: J Warwick FRICS
 Chartered Surveyors
6 Upper King Street   Tel: 0603 629621
Norwich   Fax: 0603 762299
NR3 1HA

TRANSLATIONS

Fluency - The Language   Contact: Mrs Winter
 Business
44 Great Western Terrace   Tel: 0242 250246
Cheltenham   Fax: 0242 224614
Gloucestershire
GL50 3QU

David Ackers   Contact: David Ackers
Le Faubourg
Colomby   Tel: (010 33) 3340309
50700 Valognes   Fax: (010 33) 3395141
Normandie France

TRAVEL

Brittany Ferries
Millbay Docks
Plymouth
PL1 3EW

Contact: Reservations
Office

Tel: 0752 221321